5		13
	?	
9	7	

MATHEMATICAL OLYMPIAD
CONTEST PROBLEMS

FOR CHILDREN
(ALSO FOR TEACHERS, PARENTS, AND OTHER ADULTS)

DR. GEORGE LENCHNER

$$
\begin{array}{cc}
H & E \\
H & E \\
H & E \\
+\,H & E \\
\hline
A & H \\
\end{array}
$$

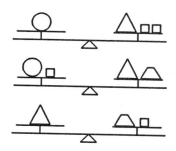

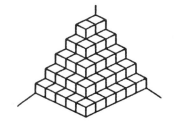

G. T. DEPARTMENT
500 MAIN STREET
EAU CLAIRE, WI 54701-3770

$$\cfrac{1}{2 + \cfrac{1}{2 + \cfrac{1}{2 + \frac{1}{2}}}}$$

About the Author

George Lenchner was formerly Director of Mathematics for the Valley Stream High School District and Consultant to three Elementary School Districts in Long Island, New York. Dr. Lenchner was the founder of the Nassau County Interscholastic Mathematics League (Mathletes) in 1955 and the Mathematical Olympiads for Elementary Schools (MOES) in 1979. Currently, he serves as the Executive Director of MOES.

Dr. Lenchner is the author of many mathematics textbooks and articles appearing in national publications. He brings to this book over forty years of experience as a mathematics teacher, supervisor, teacher-trainer, and creator of problems. He has been honored by Harvard University for Outstanding and Distinguished Secondary School Teaching.

Publisher
Glenwood Publications Inc., East Meadow, NY

Layout and Art
Aaron Bisberg, Computer Bio Center, Inc., Stamford, CT

Cover Design
Jeanne Martini, Mail Chute, Inc., Valley Stream, NY

Printer
Tobay Printing Company, Inc., Copiague, NY

Copyright © 1990 by Glenwood Publications Inc.

First Edition, printed in the United States of America. Published in New York.

All paper in this book is acid-free and meets the guidelines for permanence and durability of the Committee on Production Guidelines for Book Longevity of the Council on Library Resources.

Library of Congress Catalog Card Number: 90-083825

ISBN: 0-9626662-0-3

This book is dedicated to the
children and teachers who participate in
the Mathematical Olympiads
for Elementary Schools.

Contents

Learning to solve problems is the underlying reason for studying mathematics. It is the principal mathematical skill that needs to be developed in children.

The growth and development of calculators and computers has brought with it a different outlook on current elementary school mathematics, particularly the computational aspects of the program. In 1977, the National Council of Supervisors of Mathematics placed problem solving at the head of its list of ten basic skills of mathematics. The National Council of Teachers of Mathematics stated in their 1980 publication, *An Agenda for Action*, that problem solving must be the focus of school mathematics in the 1980s.

But developing the problem solving skill of children is dependent on finding and creating problems which will stimulate and challenge the minds of children. This book is a collection of 250 such problems. They were authored and compiled by Dr. George Lenchner for the Mathematical Olympiads for Elementary Schools, a not-for-profit tax-exempt public foundation, over the ten-year period 1979-1989. In 1989-1990, over 80,000 children representing approximately 3,000 teams, located in the U.S.A. and 21 foreign countries, participated in the Mathematical Olympiads for Elementary Schools.

An Olympiad is an interschool competition which is held five times during the school year. Each Olympiad contains five problems, each with a specified time limit. Teachers, parents, administrators, and curriculum specialists have observed that the Olympiad problems do stimulate and challenge the minds of young children in the elementary and middle school grades. This can be attributed to the appeal of the problems to reasoning, logic, ingenuity, resourcefulness, creativity, and important principles of mathematics.

It is the hope of the author that the problems in this book will:

♦ stimulate children's interest and enthusiasm for problem solving in mathematics,

♦ broaden their mathematical intuition and develop their "brain power,"

♦ introduce them to interesting and important mathematical ideas, and

♦ let them experience the fun, satisfaction, pleasure, and thrill of discovery associated with creative problem solving.

The problems in this book were reviewed by a select group of mathematicians and teachers over the ten-year period 1979-89 for ambiguity, language, and level of difficulty. Special thanks are in order for these reviewers. Their names are: Harry Sitomer (deceased), Harry Ruderman, Dr. Hamilton S. Blum, Mary D. Morrison, Gil Kessler, and Larry Zimmerman.

Introduction

Advice to the Reader on Problem Solving

Understanding the Problem

Before you try to solve a problem, make sure you understand the wording of the problem, its question, and any special words it might contain such as digit, factor, diagonal, and so forth. Does the problem give you too little, just enough, or too much information? Can you restate the problem in your own words? Can you guess what the answer will look like?

Planning to Solve the Problem

Do you have a plan of action to use in solving the problem? Such plans are called *strategies*. Here are some that are used more frequently than others:

* Find a Pattern
* Draw a Picture or Diagram
* Make an Organized List
* Make a Table
* Work Backwards
* Use Logic

More will be said about the above strategies in the next section titled *Strategies*.

Carrying out the Plan

You will observe that each problem in this book has a suggested time limit which begins after you read the problem and are ready to begin. Select a strategy from the above list or use one of your own choice. You may also want to use a combination of strategies. Now try to solve the problem. If you are not able to do the problem within the recommended time limit, continue to work on the problem until you have a solution. Speed is not important! As you become more experienced with different strategies and mathematical ideas and skills, the amount of time you need to do a problem will decrease naturally. If you experience difficulty with a computation, get help from your teacher, a parent, or another student. If your strategy doesn't seem to be working, try a different strategy. If you are still "stumped", go on to another problem. Later, you may want to again try the problem that stumped you. Perhaps you will think of a way of doing the problem in the time that elapsed. If that doesn't help, read *Using the Sections of This Book* which begins on page 16.

Introduction

Looking Back

When you get an answer, compare it to what you thought your answer might look like. Is your answer reasonable? Reread the problem and the question that is being asked. Now write your answer in a complete sentence. Compare it with the answer given in the Answer section. If you are satisfied with your answer, try to find a different strategy that could be used to solve the problem. Can you relate this problem to other problems you may have solved in the past? If you used different strategies to solve the problem, compare them and try to decide which is best for you. If you were able to solve the problem but experienced some difficulty, try it again at a later date to see if you remember how you overcame your difficulties.

Strategies

Knowledge of algebra and its associated techniques are not necessary for solving any of the Olympiad problems. Try to solve the problems non-algebraically even if you have experience in algebra. You may make some interesting discoveries involving the variables of the problem.

The following are illustrations of the strategies that are listed under Planning to Solve the Problem.

Find a Pattern

Express the following sum of fractions as a simple fraction in lowest terms:

$$\frac{1}{1\times2} + \frac{1}{2\times3} + \frac{1}{3\times4} + \frac{1}{4\times5} + \frac{1}{5\times6} + \frac{1}{6\times7} + \frac{1}{7\times8} + \frac{1}{8\times9}$$

1) Start with the first fraction; 2) add the second fraction to the first fraction and express the sum in simplest form; 3) add the third fraction to the sum of the first and second and express the sum in simplest form. Did you get the following results?

1) $$\frac{1}{1\times2} = \frac{1}{2}$$

2) $$\frac{1}{1\times2} + \frac{1}{2\times3} = \frac{2}{3}$$

3) $$\frac{1}{1\times2} + \frac{1}{2\times3} + \frac{1}{3\times4} = \frac{3}{4}$$

Check that the above equations are true. Now look for a pattern by comparing the right side of each of the above equations with the set of fractions being added to the left side. Try to answer the given question. See the next section *Solutions and Answers to Problems in Strategies*, page 12.

The strategy used above is given as an illustration of *Finding a Pattern.* Understand that there may be better ways to do this problem.

Draw a Picture or a Diagram

Four distinct lines are drawn across a rectangle. What is the maximum number of non-overlapping pieces into which the rectangle can be subdivided by these four lines

Draw a diagram of the rectangle and experiment with the placement of the four distinct lines across the rectangle.

What happens if all of the four lines intersect in one common point in or on the rectangle? What happens if the four lines do not intersect in an interior point of the rectangle? See the next section *Solutions and Answers to Problems in Strategies*, page 13.

Make an Organized List

Five students hold a checkers tournament. In the first round, each of the students plays each of the other students just once. How many different games are played?

Designate each of the students as A, B, C, D, and E. Let a pair of letters such as AB stand for the game played by A and B. Notice that AB and BA stand for the same game. Now list, in an organized way, the different games that can be played. See the next section *Solutions and Answers to Problems in Strategies*, page 14.

Make a Table

The toll for an automobile to cross a certain bridge is 40¢. A machine in an EXACT CHANGE lane will accept any combination of coins that has a total value of exactly 40¢ but will not accept pennies. In how many different ways can a driver pay the toll in an EXACT CHANGE lane?

Make a table of the different combinations of coins. Use Q, D, and N to denote the number of quarters, dimes, and nickels used in each combination having total value 40¢. See the next section *Solutions and Answers to Problems in Strategies*, page 14.

Work Backwards

I have a magic Money Box which will double any amount of money placed in it and then add \$1 to that amount. One day, I placed a certain amount of money in the Magic Money Box and got a new amount. I then placed the new amount in the Magic Money Box and got \$75. How much money did I first place in the box?

Amount placed in the box the <u>second time</u>	What the Magic Money Box did to the amount		The new amount I received
?	2 x ? + \$1	=	\$75

If I subtract \$1 from \$75, I have the double of what was placed in the Magic Money Box the second time. Then \$74 is that double. Therefore \$37 is the amount placed in the box the second time. Now repeat these operations for the first amount of money placed in the box. See the next section *Solutions and Answers to Problems in Strategies*, page 14.

Use Logic

A school has 400 students. Prove that there must be two students who have the same birthday.

Before you read ahead, try to think of how you might prove this. What do you think of the method of having each student tell you his or her birthday and then comparing the data to determine whether there is a match? Can you suggest a better method? See page 15.

$$\boxed{\textbf{Solutions and Answers to Problems in Strategies}}$$

Find a Pattern

Did you notice in the table of results how the sum on the right side of each equation is related to the last fraction on the left side ? What do you think the result will be when the fourth fraction is added to the sum of the first three fractions? Now add the fourth fraction to the sum of the first three fractions. Compare your guess to the actual sum which is 4/5. What do you think is the sum of the fractions in the given problem?

Answer: The sum of the given series of fractions is 8/9.

Draw a Picture or a Diagram

a. The maximum number of non-overlapping pieces is created when each of the four lines drawn across the rectangle intersects the other three lines in different points located in the interior of the rectangle. See the diagram below.

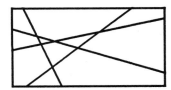

Answer: The maximum number of non-overlapping pieces is eleven.

b. Four lines drawn across the rectangle which intersect in one common point in or on the rectangle:

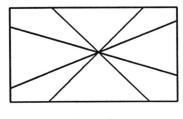
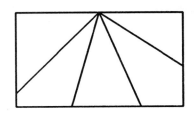

Case 1   Case 2

In case 1, the common point is in the interior of the rectangle and there are 8 subdivisions.

In case 2, the common point is on a side of the rectangle and there are 5 subdivisions.

c. Four lines drawn across the rectangle which do not intersect in an interior point of the rectangle:

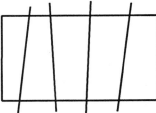

If four distinct lines are drawn across the rectangle and do not intersect in any interior point of the rectangle, there will be five non-overlapping subdivisions.

Make an Organized List

The different games that can be played are:

$$AB, \quad AC, \quad AD, \quad AE$$
$$BC, \quad BD, \quad BE$$
$$CD, \quad CE$$
$$DE$$

Notice that each pair in the first line starts with A, each pair in the second line starts with B, and so forth. Doing this makes it easier to organize the list.

Answer: The five students will play ten different games in the first round

Make a Table

	Q	D	N
1)	1	1	1
2)	1	0	3
3)	0	4	0
4)	0	3	2
5)	0	2	4
6)	0	1	6
7)	0	0	8

Notice how the table starts by using the coin of largest value, then shifts to the coin of the next-largest value, and finally to nickels. You could reverse the order of the table by starting with the coin of the smallest value.

Answer: If pennies are not used, there are seven different combinations of coins that can be used to pay a 40¢ toll in the EXACT CHANGE lane.

Work Backwards

Amount placed in the box the first time	What the Magic Money Box did to the amount		The new amount I received
?	2 x ? + $1	=	$37

If I subtract $1 from $37, I have the double of what was placed in the Magic Money Box the first time. Can you now complete the solution?

If $1 is subtracted from $37, the result is the double of what was placed in the Magic Money Box the first time. Then $36 is that double.

Answer: $18 is the amount placed in the box the first time.

Use Logic

a. There are 365 different birthdays in a year. Consider just 365 of the 400 students. If you wish to prove that 2 of these 365 students have the same birthday, then the worst thing that could happen to you is for each of the 365 students to have a birthday which is different from the others. But any one of the remaining 35 students of the 400 must have a birthday which matches one of the 365 different birthdays.

Conclusion: In a group of 400 students, there must be at least one pair of students with the same birthday.

Here are some additional questions for you to consider with reference to the given problem.

b. Find the smallest number of different pairs of the 400 students such that each pair has the same birthday.

Suppose each of 365 students has a birthday which differs from the others. Then each of remaining 35 students has a birthday which matches one of the 365 different birthdays. If each of the remaining 35 students has a birthday different from the other 34 students, then there will be 35 different pairs of students that have the same birthday.

c. Again suppose that 365 of 400 students each has a birthday different from the others. What is the largest number of pairs that can have the same birthday?

Suppose student X in the group of 365 students has her birthday on May 1. Suppose further that students A and B in the group of the remaining 35 students also have birthdays on May 1. Then the following pairs have the same birthday: AX, BX, and AB. In section a. above when A and B had different birthdays, they each could be matched only once and thus accounted for just two different pairs. When they had the same birthday, they accounted for 3 different pairs. If we add student C with the same birthday as A and B, we will obtain the following pairs having the same birthday:

XA,	XB,	XC
AB,	AC	
BC		

Suppose all 35 students have the same birthday which, of course, must match one of the 365 different birthdays. Thus there are 36 students who have the same birthday. If we try to count all of the different pairs who have the same birthday by the above method, it will take a lot of effort and time. Let us use logic.

Take the 36 students in any order and designate them as the first student, the second student, the third student, and so forth up to the thirty-sixth student. The first student can be matched with each of the remaining 35 students to form a pair; the second student can be matched with each of the 35 remaining students; the third student can be matched with each of the remaining 35 students; and so forth up to the thirty-sixth student who also can be matched with each of the remaining 35 students. The total of all these matches is 36x35. But have any of the matches been counted more than once? For example, consider the match of the first student with the eighth student. Will that match occur again in the total of 36x35 matches? Yes, it will occur again when we consider the eighth student being matched with each of the remaining 35 students. So you see that each match will occur twice in the total of 36x35 matches. To determine the correct number of different matches, what must we do to 36x35? Do you agree that we should divide by 2?

$$\frac{36 \times 35}{2} = 630$$

When 365 of 400 students have different birthdays, the largest number of different pairs of students which have the same birthday occurs when the remaining 35 students have the same birthday. In this case, the largest number of different pairs of students which have the same birthday is 630.

Using the Different Sections of This Book

In addition to the Olympiad problems of this book, there are three other sections which will be helpful to you. The sections are titled: *Answers*; *Hints*; and *Solutions*. The following describes how to use the three sections so that your ability to solve problems will improve, your knowledge of mathematics will expand, and your enjoyment of mathematics will grow.

When You Have a Solution

Check your answer against the answer given in the *Answers* section.

1) If the answers agree, compare the strategy you selected with the strategies given in the *Solutions*. Study the strategies that are different than yours. Try to decide which strategy is most efficient, which is most easily understood, and which is best or you at your stage of mathematical development.

2) If the answers do not agree, go over your work carefully. You may have made an error in computation or in copying the given information onto your paper. If you decide that you have not made either of the errors described in the preceding sentence, read the reference for the problem in *Hints*. Redo the problem using one or more of the ideas suggested in *Hints*. Remember to again compare your answer with the given answer.

Introduction

When You Do Not Have a Strategy for Solution

Read the reference to the problem in *Hints*.

1) If you are now able to obtain a solution, proceed as indicated above.

2) If *Hints* does not help you, go to *Solutions* and cover the solution of the problem with a sheet of paper. Reveal and read one line at a time until you think you can proceed on your own. If you are not able to proceed on your own, go over the given solutions. Select the one you understand best and study it. Write that solution without referring to *Solutions*. At a later date, say a week or two, try to redo the problem without referring to *Solutions*. This will show how much you have retained and learned.

Sharing the Problems

The Olympiad problems will stimulate your imagination and challenge your resourcefulness and ingenuity. You may also discover that reading the problems from time to time will be an enjoyable experience and will strengthen your problem solving skill. Share the problems with your classmates, friends, teachers and parents. They too may find the problems interesting and challenging.

Your Score on Each Olympiad

You can use the following scale to evaluate your problem solving ability for each Olympiad of five problems.

Number of Correct Answers	Rating
5	excellent
4	superior
3	very good
2	good
1	average
0	try again

Remember -- learning how to solve problems is more important than having a correct answer.

Olympiads

1.
4 Min.

Suppose today is Tuesday.

What day of the week will it be 100 days from now?

2.
5 Min.

I have four 3¢-stamps and three 5¢-stamps.

Using one or more of these stamps, how many different amounts of postage can I make?

3.
5 Min.

Find the sum of the counting numbers from 1 to 25 inclusive.

In other words, if S = 1 + 2 + 3 + ... + 24 + 25, find the value of S.

4.
5 Min.

In a stationery store, pencils have one price and pens have another price. Two pencils and three pens cost 78¢. But three pencils and two pens cost 72¢.

How much does one pencil cost?

5.
5 Min.

A work crew of 3 people requires 3 weeks and 2 days to do a certain job.

How long would it take a work crew of 4 people to do the same job if each person of both crews works at the same rate as each of the others? Note: each week contains six work days.

1. 5 Min.	A girl bought a dog for $10, sold it for $15, bought it back for $20, and finally sold it for $25.
	Did the girl make or lose money, and how much did she make or lose?

2. 5 Min.	I have 30 coins consisting of nickels and quarters. The total value of the coins is $4.10.
	How many of each kind do I have?

3. 5 Min.	Rectangular cards, 2 inches by 3 inches, are cut from a rectangular sheet 2 feet by 3 feet.
	What is the greatest number of cards that can be cut from the sheet?

4. 5 Min.	In three bowling games, Alice scores 139, 143, and 144.
	What score will Alice need in a fourth game in order to have an average score of 145 for all four games?

5. 5 Min.	A book has 500 pages numbered 1, 2, 3, and so on.
	How many times does the digit 1 appear in the page numbers?

1.
5 Min.

A set of marbles can be divided in equal shares among 2, 3, 4, 5, or 6 children with no marbles left over.

What is the least number of marbles that the set could have?

2.
5 Min.

A motorist made a 60-mile trip averaging 20 miles per hour. On the return trip, he averaged 30 miles per hour.

What was the motorist's average speed for the entire trip?

3.
5 Min.

The four-digit numeral 3AA1 is divisible by 9.

What digit does A represent?

4.
5 Min.

Consider the following sum:

$$\frac{1}{1 \times 2} + \frac{1}{2 \times 3} + \frac{1}{3 \times 4} + \frac{1}{4 \times 5} + \frac{1}{5 \times 6}$$

Express the sum as a simple fraction in lowest terms.

5.
5 Min.

If we count by 3s starting with 1, the following sequence is obtained: 1, 4, 7, 10, . . .

What is the 100th number in the sequence?

| 1.
5 Min.	100 pounds of chocolate is packaged into boxes each containing 1¼ pounds of chocolate. Each box is then sold for $1.75.
	What is the total selling price for all of the boxes of chocolate?

| 2.
5 Min.	In the multiplication problem at the right, A and B stand for different digits.	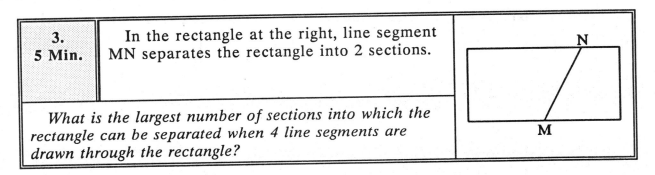
Find A and B.		

| 3.
5 Min.	In the rectangle at the right, line segment MN separates the rectangle into 2 sections.	
What is the largest number of sections into which the rectangle can be separated when 4 line segments are drawn through the rectangle?		

| 4.
5 Min.	Given: $\dfrac{1}{3} = \dfrac{1}{A} + \dfrac{1}{B}$ where A and B are different whole numbers.
What are the values of A and B?	

| 5.
5 Min.	P and Q represent numbers, and P * Q means $\dfrac{P+Q}{2}$.
*What is the value of 3 * (6 * 8)?*	

1.
5 Min.
The numbers 2, 4, 6, and 8 are a set of four consecutive even numbers. Suppose the sum of five consecutive even numbers is 320.

What is the smallest of the five numbers?

2.
5 Min.
Amy can mow 600 square yards of grass in 1½ hours.

At this rate, how many minutes would it take her to mow 600 square feet?

3.
5 Min.
Given the fraction in the box to the right.

Express the fraction as a simple fraction in lowest terms.

$$\cfrac{1}{2 + \cfrac{1}{2 + \cfrac{1}{2 + \cfrac{1}{2}}}}$$

4.
5 Min.
There are many numbers that divide 109 with a remainder of 4.

List all two-digit numbers that have that property.

5.
5 Min.
A dealer packages marbles in two different box sizes. One size holds 5 marbles and the other size holds 12 marbles.

If the dealer packaged 99 marbles and used more than 10 boxes, how many boxes of each size did he use?

1.
3 Min.
X and Y are two different numbers selected from the first fifty counting numbers from 1 to 50 inclusive.

What is the largest value that $\dfrac{X+Y}{X-Y}$ can have?

2.
5 Min.
A chime clock strikes 1 chime at one o'clock, 2 chimes at two o'clock, 3 chimes at three o'clock, and so forth.

What is the total number of chimes the clock will strike in a twelve-hour period?

3.
4 Min.
The average of five weights is 13 grams. This set of five weights is increased by another weight of 7 grams.

What is the average of the six weights?

4.
6 Min.
From a pile of 100 pennies, 100 nickels, and 100 dimes, select 21 coins which have a total value of exactly $1.00. In your selection you must also use at least one coin of each type.

How many coins of each of the three types should be selected?

5.
5 Min.
In a group of 30 high school students, 8 take French, 12 take Spanish and 3 take both languages.

How many students of the group take neither French nor Spanish?

1.
4 Min.

A palimage of a natural number is the number which has the same digits but in reverse order. For example, 659 and 956 are palimages; so are 1327 and 7231. Now add 354 and its palimage. Call this sum X. Add X and its palimage. Call this sum Y. Add Y and its palimage. Call this sum Z.

What is the value of Z?

2.
5 Min.

A boy has the following seven coins in his pocket: 2 pennies, 2 nickels, 2 dimes, and 1 quarter. He takes out two coins, records the sum of their values, and then puts them back with the other coins. He continues to take out two coins, records the sum of their values, and puts them back with the other coins.

How many different sums can he record at most?

3.
4 Min.

Suppose all the counting numbers are arranged in columns as shown at the right.

A	B	C	D	E	F	G
1	2	3	4	5	6	7
8	9	10	11	12	13	14
15	16	—	—	—	—	—
—	—	—	—	—	—	—

Under what letter will the number 1000 appear?

4.
4 Min.

Twelve people purchased supplies for a ten-day camping trip with the understanding that each of the twelve will get equal daily shares. They are then joined by three more people, but make no further purchases.

How long will the supplies then last if the original daily share for each person is not changed?

5.
5 Min.

The U-shaped figure at the right contains 11 squares of the same size. The area of the U-shaped figure is 176 square inches.

How many inches are there in the perimeter of the U-shaped figure?

1. 4 Min.	A bag contains 500 beads, each of the same size, but in 5 different colors. Suppose there are 100 beads of each color and I am blindfolded.

What is the least number of beads I must pick before I can be sure there are 5 beads of the same color among the beads I have picked blindfolded?

2. 5 Min.	If 20 is added to one-third of a number, the result is the double of the number.

What is the number?

3. 5 Min.	Each of the boxes in the figure at the right is a square.

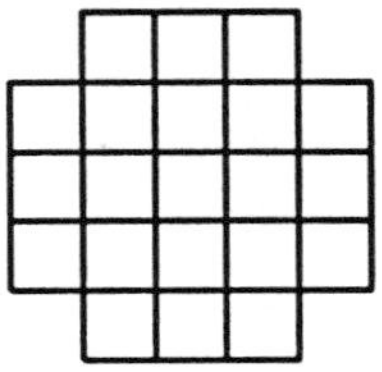

How many different squares can be traced using the lines in the figure?

4. 5 Min.	A woman spent two-thirds of her money. She lost two-thirds of the remainder and then had $4 left.

With how much money did she start?

5. 5 Min.	If a number ends in zeros, the zeros are called *terminal zeros*. For example, 520,000 has four terminal zeros, but 502,000 has just three terminal zeros. Let N equal the product of all natural numbers from 1 through 20: N = 1 x 2 x 3 x 4 x . . . x 20.

How many terminal zeros will N have when it is written in standard form?

1.
5 Min.

In the "magic-square" at the right, five more numbers can be placed in the boxes so that the sum of the three numbers in each row, in each column, and in each diagonal is always the same.

15		35
50		
25	X	

*What value should **X** have?*

2.
3 Min.

If I start with 2 and count by 3's until I reach 449, I will get: 2, 5, 8, 11, . . . , 449 where 2 is the first number, 5 is the second number, 8 is the third number and so forth.

If 449 is the Nth number, what is the value of N?

3.
5 Min.

The perimeter of a rectangle is 22 inches and the inch-measure of each side is a natural number.

How many different areas in square inches can the rectangle have?

4.
5 Min.

A man drives from his home at 30 miles per hour to the shopping center which is 20 miles from his home. On the return trip he encounters heavy traffic and averages 12 miles per hour.

How much time does the man take in driving to and from the shopping center?

5.
5 Min.

In the division problem at the right, the blanks represent missing digits.

$$
\begin{array}{r}
A\ B \\
5\ \_\ \overline{)\ \_\ \_\ \_} \\
\underline{\ \_\ \overline{6}\ \_} \\
\overline{4\ 3\ \_} \\
\underline{\hspace{2em}0}
\end{array}
$$

If A and B represent the digits of the quotient, what are the values of A and B?

1. **3 Min.**	In the addition problem at the right, each letter stands for a digit and different letters stand for different digits.	H E H E H E + H E A H
	What digits do the letters H, E, *and* A *each represent?*	

---

2. **5 Min.**	The product of two numbers is 144 and their difference is 10.
	What is the sum of the two numbers?

---

3. **5 Min.**	A and B are whole numbers, and $$\frac{A}{11} + \frac{B}{3} = \frac{31}{33}$$
	Find A *and* B.

---

4. **5 Min.**	The XYZ club collected a total of $1.21 from its members with each member contributing the same amount.
	If each member paid for his or her share with 3 coins, how many nickels were contributed?

---

5. **5 Min.**	During a school year, a student was given an award of 25¢ for each math test he passed and was fined 50¢ for each math test he failed. At the end of the school year, the student had passed 7 times as many tests as he had failed, and received $3.75.
	How many tests did he fail?

1.
5 Min.

Julius Caesar wrote the Roman Numerals I, II, III, IV, and V in a certain order from left to right. He wrote I before III but after IV. He wrote II after IV but before I. He wrote V after II but before III.

If V was not the third numeral, in what order did Caesar write the five numerals from left to right?.

2.
5 Min.

In the multiplication problem at the right, each blank space represents a missing digit.

Find the product.

```
    4 _ _
  ×   _ 7
  _____
      8 2
  1 _2 _ _
```

3.
4 Min.

Glen, Harry, and Kim each have a different favorite sport among tennis, baseball, and soccer. Glen does not like baseball or soccer. Harry does not like baseball.

Name the favorite sport of each person.

4.
4 Min.

An acute angle is an angle whose measure is between 0° and 90°.

Using the rays in the diagram, how many different acute angles can be formed?

5.
5 Min.

Thirteen plums weigh as much as two apples and one pear. Four plums and one apple have the same weight as one pear.

How many plums have the weight of one pear?

| 1.
4 Min. | Arrange the digits 1, 1, 2, 2, 3, 3, as a six-digit number in which the 1s are separated by one digit, the 2s are separated by two digits, and the 3s are separated by three digits. |

There are two answers. Find one.

| 2.
3 Min. | Suppose five days before the day after tomorrow was Wednesday. |

What day of the week was yesterday?

| 3.
5 Min. | In the diagram at the right, ABCD is a square whose sides are each 2 units long. The length of the shortest path from A to C following the lines of the diagram is 4 units. | 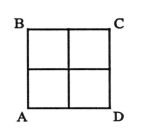 |

How many different shortest paths are there from A to C?

| 4.
5 Min. | A dollar was changed into 16 coins consisting of just nickels and dimes. |

How many coins of each kind were in the change?

| 5.
4 Min. | A number has a remainder of 1 when divided by 4, a remainder of 2 when divided by 5, and a remainder of 3 when divided by 6. |

What is the smallest number that has the above properties?

1.
4 Min.

Each of the boxes in the figure at the right is a square.

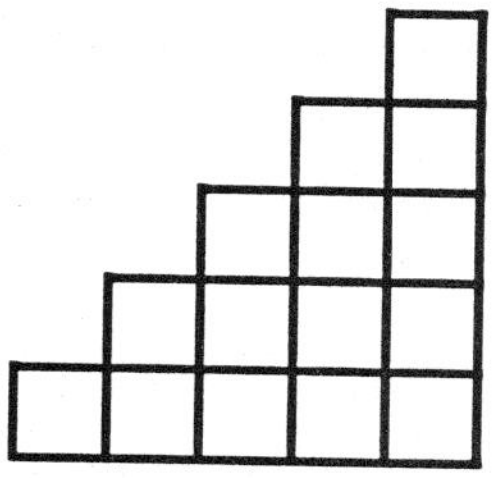

Using the lines of the figure, how many different squares can be traced?

2.
5 Min.

In the multiplication problem at the right, different letters stand for different digits, and ABC and DBC each represent a three-digit number.

$$
\begin{array}{r}
A\ B\ C \\
C \\
\hline
D\ B\ C
\end{array}
$$

What number does DBC represent? (Two answers are possible; give one.)

3.
4 Min.

Consecutive numbers are whole numbers that follow in order such as 7, 8, 9, 10, 11, and 12.

Find three consecutive numbers such that the sum of the first and third is 118.

4.
6 Min.

When Anne, Betty, and Cynthia compared the amount of money each had, they discovered that Anne and Betty together had $12, Betty and Cynthia together had $18, and Anne and Cynthia together had $10.

Who had the least amount of money, and how much was it?

5.
5 Min.

A total of fifteen pennies are put into four piles so that each pile has a different number of pennies.

What is the smallest possible number of pennies in the largest pile?

1.
4 Min.
The perimeter of a rectangle is 20 feet and the foot-measure of each side is a whole number.

How many rectangles with different shapes satisfy these conditions?

2.
4 Min.
In a math contest of 10 problems, 5 points was given for each correct answer and 2 points was deducted for each incorrect answer.

If Nancy did all 10 problems and scored 29 points, how many correct answers did she have?

3.
4 Min.
The counting numbers are arranged in four columns as shown at the right.

A	B	C	D
1	2	3	4
8	7	6	5
9	10	11	12
. . . . .		14	13

In which column will 101 appear?

4.
6 Min.
Three water pipes are used to fill a swimming pool. The first pipe alone takes 8 hours to fill the pool, the second pipe alone takes 12 hours to fill the pool, and the third pipe alone takes 24 hours to fill the pool.

If all three pipes are opened at the same time, how long will it take to fill the pool?

5.
5 Min.
In the magic square at the right, the four numbers in each column, in each row, and in each of the two diagonals, have the same sum.

		7	12
N	4	9	
	5	16	3
8	11		

What value should N have?

1.
5 Min.

A train can hold 78 passengers. The train starts out empty and picks up 1 passenger at the first stop, 2 passengers at the second stop, 3 passengers at the third stop, and so forth.

After how many stops will the train be full?

2.
5 Min.

The outside of a wooden 4 inch cube is painted red. The painted cube is then cut into 1 inch cubes.

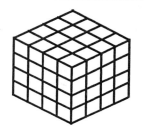

How many of the 1 inch cubes do not have red paint on any face?

3.
5 Min.

The number of two-dollar bills I need to pay for a purchase is 9 more than the number of five-dollar bills I need to pay for the same purchase.

What is the cost of the purchase?

4.
4 Min.

If 24 gallons of water are poured into an empty tank, then 3/4 of the tank is filled.

How many gallons does a full tank hold?

5.
6 Min.

3x3, 3x3x3, and 3x3x3x3 are multiplication strings of two 3s, three 3s, and four 3s respectively. When each string multiplication is done, 3x3 ends in 9, 3x3x3 ends in 7, and 3x3x3x3 ends in 1.

If a multiplication string of thirty-five 3's is done, in what digit will it end?

1.
2 Min.

The last Friday of a particular month is on the 25th day of the month.

What day of the week is the first day of the month?

2.
4 Min.

The age of a man is the same as his wife's age with the digits reversed. The sum of their ages is 99 and the man is 9 years older than his wife.

How old is the man?

3.
4 Min.

A group of 21 people went to the county fair either in a stagecoach or in buggies. Later the same stagecoach and buggies brought them back. On the trip to the fair, 9 people rode in the stagecoach and 3 people rode in each buggy.

On the return trip, how many people rode in the stagecoach if 4 people rode in each buggy?

4.
5 Min.

Below are three views of the same cube.

What letter is on the face opposite (1) H, (2) X, and (3) Y? (Give your answer in the same order.)

5.
5 Min.

D is the sum of the odd numbers from 1 through 99 inclusive, and N is the sum of the even numbers from 2 through 98 inclusive:
D = 1 + 3 + 5 + . . . + 99 and N = 2 + 4 + 6 + . . . + 98

Which is greater, D or N, and by how much?

1.
3 Min.

I have exactly ten coins whose total value is $1.

If three of the coins are quarters, what are the remaining coins?

2.
4 Min.

One loaf of bread and six rolls cost $1.80. At the same prices, two loaves of bread and four rolls cost $2.40.

How much does one loaf of bread cost?

3.
5 Min.

The small boxes in Figures A and B at the right are congruent squares.

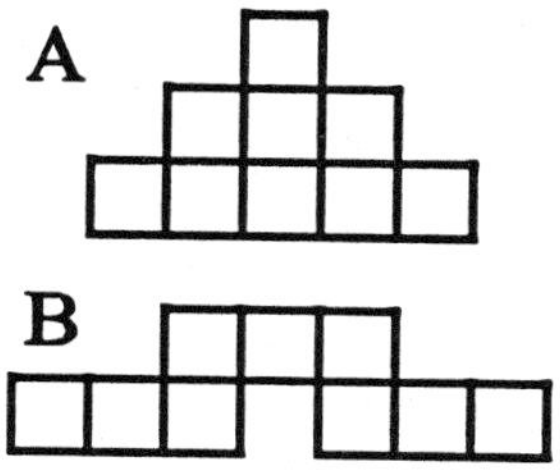

If the perimeter of Figure A is 48 inches, what is the perimeter of Figure B? (The perimeter of a figure is the distance around it.)

A

B

4.
5 Min.

If a kindergarten teacher places her children 4 on each bench, there will be 3 children who will not have a place. However, if 5 children are placed on each bench, there will be 2 empty places.

What is the smallest number of children the class could have?

5.
4 Min.

If the digits A, B, and C are added, the sum is the two-digit number AB as shown at the right.

What is the value of C?

$$\begin{array}{r} A \\ B \\ + C \\ \hline A\,B \end{array}$$

1.
4 Min.

The sum of the weights of Tom and Bill is 138 pounds and one boy is 34 pounds heavier than the other.

How much does the heavier boy weigh?

2.
5 Min.

When I open my mathematics book, there are two pages which face me and the product of the two page numbers is 1806.

What are the two page numbers?

3.
4 Min.

Eight one-inch cubes are put together to form the T-figure shown at the right. The complete outside of the T-figure is painted red and then separated into one-inch cubes.

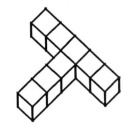

How many of the cubes have exactly four red faces?

4.
5 Min.

The members of an Olympiad team contributed a total of $1.69 for refreshments for their weekly practice. Each member contributed the same amount and paid for his or her share in five coins.

How many nickels were contributed by all of the members?

5.
5 Min.

Consecutive numbers are counting numbers that follow in order as in 7, 8, 9, 10, and so forth. Suppose the average of 15 consecutive numbers is 15.

What is the average of the first five numbers of the set?

1. 2 Min.	A camera and case together cost $100.
	If the camera costs $90 more than the case, how much does the case cost?

2. 3 Min.	In the addition problem at the right A, B, and C are digits. If C is placed in the tens column instead of the units column as shown at the far right, the sum is 97.	$\begin{array}{r} A\ B \\ +\ \ C \\ \hline 5\ 2 \end{array}$	$\begin{array}{r} A\ B \\ +\ C \\ \hline 9\ 7 \end{array}$
	What are the values of A, B, and C?		

3. 5 Min.	Suppose K, L, and M represent the number of points assigned to the three target regions shown at the right. The sum of K and L is 11, the sum of L and M is 19, and the sum of K and M is 16.	
	How many points are assigned to M?	

4. 5 Min.	Mrs. Winthrop went to a store, spent half of her money and then $10 more. She went to a second store, spent half of her remaining money and then $10 more. But she then had no money left.
	How much money did she have to begin with when she went to the first store?

5. 5 Min.	A4273B is a six-digit number in which A and B are digits.
	If the number is divisible by 72 without remainder, what values do A and B have?

1.
4 Min.

A train is moving at the rate of 1 mile in 1 minute and 20 seconds.

If the train continues at this rate, how far will it travel in one hour?

2.
4 Min.

If a number is divided by 3 or 5, the remainder is 1. If it is divided by 7, there is no remainder.

What number between 1 and 100 satisfies the above conditions?

3.
5 Min.

Train cars made of blocks of wood either 6 inches long or 7 inches long can be hooked together to make longer trains.

Which of the following train-lengths cannot be made by hooking together either 6-inch train cars, 7-inch train cars, or a combination of both:
29 inches, 30 inches, 31 inches, 32 inches, 33 inches?

4.
5 Min.

A circular track is 1000 yards in circumference. Cyclists A, B, and C race around the track: A at the rate of 700 yards per minute, B at the rate of 800 yards per minute, and C at the rate of 900 yards per minute.

If they start from the same position at the same time and cycle in the same direction, what is the least number of minutes it must take before all three are together again?

5.
5 Min.

Alice and Betty each want to buy the same kind of ruler. But Alice is 22¢ short and Betty is 3¢ short. When they combine their money, they still do not have enough money.

What is the most the ruler could cost?

1. **4 Min.**	Six dollars were exchanged for nickels and dimes. The number of nickels was the same as the number of dimes.

How many nickels were there in the change?

2. **4 Min.**	In the multiplication example at the right, A, B, and H represent different digits.	B A 7 ——— H A A

What is the sum of A, B, and H?

3. **5 Min.**	A total of 350 pounds of cheese is packaged into boxes each containing 1¾ pounds of cheese. Each box is then sold for $1.75.

What is the total selling price of all of the boxes of cheese?

4. **4 Min.**	A wooden block is 4 inches long, 4 inches wide, and 1 inch high. The block is painted red on all six sides and then cut into sixteen 1 inch cubes.	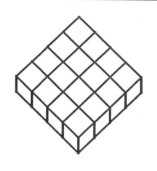

How many of the cubes each have a total number of red faces that is an even number?

5. **6 Min.**	$1200 is divided among four brothers so that each gets $100 more than the brother who is his next younger brother.

How much does the youngest brother get?

| **1.**
3 Min. | Suppose two days ago was Sunday. |

What day of the week will 365 days from today then be?

| **2.**
5 Min. | 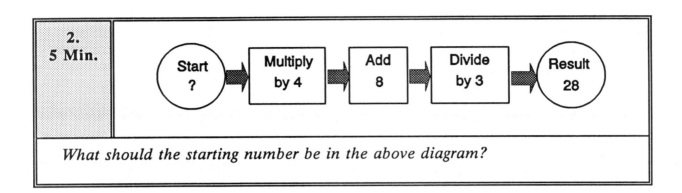 |

What should the starting number be in the above diagram?

| **3.**
5 Min. | A rectangular tile is 2 inches by 3 inches. |

What is the least number of tiles that are needed to completely cover a square region 2 feet on each side?

| **4.**
6 Min. | Six arrows land on the target shown at the right. Each arrow is in one of the regions of the target. |

Which of the following total scores is possible:
16, 19, 26, 31, 41, 44?

| **5.**
6 Min. | A number N divides each of 17 and 30 with the same remainder in each case. |

What is the largest value N can have?

1. 4 Min.	The average of five numbers is 18. Let the first number be increased by 1, the second number by 2, the third number by 3, the fourth number by 4, and the fifth number by 5.

What is the average of the set of increased numbers?

2. 5 Min.	The set of stairs shown at the right is constructed by placing layers of cubes on top of each other.	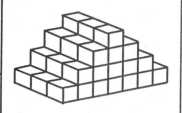

What is the total number of cubes contained in the staircase?

3. 6 Min.	When a natural number is multiplied by itself, the result is a square number. Some examples of square numbers are: 1, 4, 9, 16, 25.

How many square numbers are there between 1,000 and 2,000?

4. 5 Min.	The owner of a bicycle store had a sale on bicycles (two-wheelers) and tricycles (three-wheelers). When he counted the total number of pedals of the cycles on sale, he got 50. When he counted the total number of wheels of the cycles on sale, he got 64.

How many tricycles were offered in the sale? (Note: each cycle has two pedals.)

5. 5 Min.	A jar filled with water weighs 10 pounds. When one-half of the water is poured out, the jar and remaining water weigh 5¾ pounds.

How much does the jar weigh?

1.
3 Min.

Person A was born on January 15, 1948.
Person B was born on January 15, 1962.

If both are alive now, in what year was person A twice as old as person B?

2.
5 Min.

A square piece of paper is folded in half as shown and then cut into two rectangles along the fold. The perimeter of each of the two rectangles is 18 inches.

What is the perimeter of the original square?

3.
5 Min.

In the division example at the right A and B represent different digits.

What is the sum of A and B if the remainder is zero?

```
         B A
A B / _ _ _ _
      _ _ _
        _ _ 1
      _ _ _
```

4.
5 Min.

The product of two whole numbers is 10,000.

If neither number contains a zero digit, what are the numbers?

5.
6 Min.

A train traveling at 30 miles per hour reaches a tunnel which is 9 times as long as the train.

If the train takes 2 minutes to clear the tunnel, how long is the train?
(1 mile = 5,280 feet)

1.
4 Min.

My age this year is a multiple of 7. Next year it will be a multiple of 5. I am more than 20 years of age but less than 80.

How old will I be 6 years from now?

2.
5 Min.

Six people participated in a checker tournament. Each participant played exactly three games with each of the other participants.

How many games were played in all?

3.
6 Min.

Consecutive numbers are natural numbers that follow in order as in the case of 3, 4, 5, 6, and 7.

Find three consecutive numbers whose product is 15,600.

4.
5 Min.

Of three numbers, two are $\frac{1}{2}$ and $\frac{1}{3}$.

What should the third number be so that the average of all three is 1?

5.
6 Min.

The four-digit number A 5 5 B is divisible by 36 without remainder.

What is the sum of A and B?

1. **4 Min.**	The month of January has 31 days. Suppose January 1 occurs on Monday.
	What day of the week is February 22 of the next month?

2. **5 Min.**	The diagram at the right consists of X's.	XXXXXXXXXXXXXXXXXX XXXXXXXXXX XX XXXXXXXXXX XX XXXX XXXXX XX XXX XXXXXXXXXXX XX XXXXXXXXXX XXXXXXXXXXXXXXXXXX XXXXXXXXXXXXXXXXX
	How many X's are there?	

3. **4 Min.**	The product of three natural numbers is 24.
	How many different sets of 3 numbers have this property if the order of the 3 numbers in a set does not matter?

4. **4 Min.**	A group of 12 girl scouts had enough food to last for 8 days when they arrived in camp. However, 4 more scouts joined them without the amount of food being increased.
	How long will the food last if each scout is given the same daily ration as originally planned?

5. **5 Min.**	Let N be a number that divides 171 with a remainder of 6.
	List all the two-digit numbers that N can be.

1.
3 Min.

Carol spent exactly $1 for some 5¢-stamps and some 13¢-stamps.

How many 5¢-stamps did she buy?

2.
5 Min.

A square has an area of 144 square inches. Suppose the square is partitioned into six congruent rectangles as shown at the right.

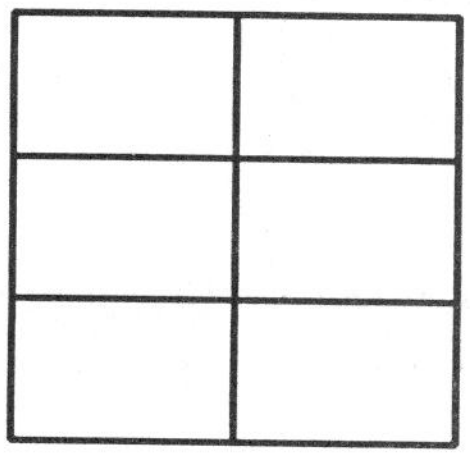

How many inches are there in the perimeter of one of the six rectangles?

3.
5 Min.

In the addition problem at the right, there are three two-digit numbers in which different letters represent different digits.

What digits do A, B, and C represent?

```
  A A
  B B
+ C C
-----
B A C
```

4.
5 Min.

The result of multiplying a natural number by itself is a square number. For example 1, 4, 9, and 16 are each square numbers because 1x1 = 1, 2x2 = 4, 3x3 = 9, and 4x4 = 16.

What year in the 20th century was a square number?

5.
4 Min.

The digits of a two-digit number are interchanged to form a new two-digit number. The difference of the original number and the new number is 45.

Find the largest two-digit number which satisfies these conditions.

| 1.
3 Min. | A and B are two different numbers selected from the first forty counting numbers (1 through 40 inclusive). |

What is the largest value that the following expression can have?

$$\frac{A \times B}{A - B}$$

| 2.
6 Min. | A twelve-hour clock loses 1 minute every hour. Suppose it shows the correct time now. |

What is the least number of hours from now when it will again show the correct time?

| 3.
5 Min. | A certain natural number is divisible by 3 and also by 5. When the number is divided by 7, the remainder is 4. |

What is the smallest number that satisfies these conditions,

| 4.
5 Min. | The figure shown consists of 3 layers of cubes with no gaps. Suppose the complete exterior of the figure is painted red and then separated into individual cubes. | 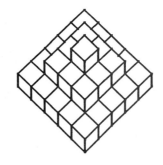 |

How many of these cubes have exactly 3 red faces?

| 5.
6 Min. | Alice needs one hour to do a certain job. Betty, her older sister, can do the same job in 1/2 hour. |

How many minutes will it take them to do the job if they work together at the given rates?

1.
4 Min.

3, 6, 9, 12, . . . are some multiples of 3.

How many multiples of 3 are there between 10 and 226?

2.
5 Min.

ABCD is a rectangle with area equal to 36 square units. Points E, F, and G are midpoints of the sides on which they are located.

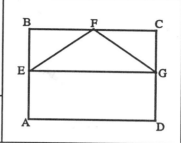

How many square units are there in the area of triangle EFG?

3.
4 Min.

When the sum of two whole numbers is multiplied by the difference of the numbers, the result is 85.

If the difference of the two numbers is not 1, what is their sum?

4.
5 Min.

30! represents the product of all natural numbers from 1 through 30 inclusive:

$$1 \times 2 \times 3 \times 4 \times 5 \times \ldots \times 28 \times 29 \times 30$$

If the product is factored into primes, how many 5s will the factorization contain?

5.
6 Min.

A printer has to number the pages of a book from 1 to 150. Suppose the printer uses a separate piece of type for each digit in each number.

How many pieces of type will the printer have to use?

Olympiad 30

1. **3 Min.**	Many whole numbers between 10 and 1,000 have 2 or 7 as the units digit?

How many such numbers are there between 10 and 1,000?

2. **3 Min.**	Peter has one of each of the following coins in his pocket: a penny, a nickel, a dime, a quarter, and a half-dollar. Four of these coins are taken out of the pocket and the sum of their values is calculated.

How many different sums are possible?

3. **4 Min.**	The front wheel of a vehicle has a circumference of 3 feet, the rear wheel has a circumference of 4 feet.

How many more complete turns will the front wheel make than the rear wheel in travelling a distance of 1 mile on a straight road? (1 mile = 5280 feet)

| **4.**<br>**6 Min.** | In the multiplication example at the right, each of A, B, and C stands for a different digit and each of the blank spaces represents a non-zero digit. | ```
  A B C
  A B C
 ──────
  _ _ _ 9
  _ _ _ 4
_ _ _ 1
──────────
``` |
| *What digits do A, B, and C each represent?* | |

5. **5 Min.**	Ann gave Betty as many cents as Betty had. Betty then gave Ann as many cents as Ann then had. At this point, each had 12 cents.

How much did Ann have at the beginning?

50
```

1.
3 Min.
The weight of a whole brick is the same as 4 pounds plus the weight of 1/3 of the whole brick.

How many pounds does the whole brick weigh?

2.
4 Min.
Consecutive odd numbers are odd numbers that differ by 2 and follow in order such as 1, 3, 5, 7, 9, or, 17, 19, 21.

Find the first of seven consecutive odd numbers if the average of the seven numbers is 41.

3.
5 Min.
When the order of the digits of 2552 is reversed, the number remains the same.

How many counting numbers between 100 and 1000 remain the same when the order of the number's digits is reversed?

4.
5 Min.
A tractor wheel is 88 inches in circumference.

How many complete turns will the wheel make in rolling one mile on the ground? (1 mile = 5,280 feet)

5.
5 Min.
In the addition problem at the right, each letter represents a digit and different letters represent different digits.

What four-digit number does D E E R represent?

```
    I N
+ R I D
-------
D E E R
```

1. **4 Min.**	Tom *multiplied* a number by 2½ and got 50 as an answer. However, he should have *divided* the number by 2½ to get the correct answer.

What is the correct answer?

2. **5 Min.**	Consider the counting numbers from 1 to 1000: 1, 2, 3, 4, . . . , 1000

Which one of these numbers, when multiplied by itself, is closest to 1985?

3. **6 Min.**	The sum of the ages of Al and Bill is 25; the sum of the ages of Al and Carl is 20; the sum of the ages of Bill and Carl is 31.

Who is the oldest of the three and how old is he?

4. **6 Min.**	A square is divided into three congruent rectangles as shown at the right. Each of the three rectangles has a perimeter of 16 meters.

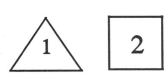

How many meters are in the perimeter of the square?

5. **6 Min.**	Abracadabra has four different coins with values as shown at the right. Suppose you had just one of each of the four different coins.

How many different amounts can be made using one or more of the coins?

1.
4 Min.
The weight of a glass bowl and the marbles it contains is 50 ounces. If the number of marbles in the bowl is doubled, the total weight of the bowl and marbles is 92 ounces.

What is the weight of the bowl? (Assume that each of the marbles has the same weight.)

2.
5 Min.
A number is greater than 10 and has the property that, when divided either by 5 or by 7, the remainder is 1.

What is the smallest odd counting number that has this property?

3.
6 Min.
The tower at the right is made up of five horizontal layers of cubes with no gaps.

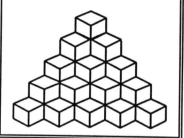

How many individual cubes are in the tower?

4.
6 Min.
A certain slow clock loses 15 minutes every hour. Suppose the clock is set to the correct time at 9 A.M.

What will the correct time be when the slow clock first shows 10 A.M.?

5.
6 Min.
Said Anne to Betty: "If you give me one marble, we will each have the same number of marbles." Said Betty to Anne: "If you give me one marble, I will have twice as many marbles as you will then have."

How many marbles did Anne have before any exchange was made?

1. 5 Min.	The sum of the first twenty-five natural numbers is 325: $$1 + 2 + 3 + 4 + \ldots + 25 = 325.$$
	What is the sum of the next twenty-five natural numbers: $$26 + 27 + 28 + 29 + \ldots + 50 = ?$$

2. 5 Min.	Eric has just three types of coins in his change-purse: nickels, dimes, and quarters. The purse contains more dimes than quarters, and more quarters than nickels and there are seven coins in all.
	What is the total value of the seven coins?

3. 6 Min.	Square ABCD and rectangle AEFG each have an area of 36 square meters. E is the midpoint of AB.	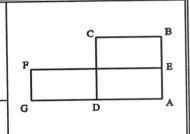
	What is the perimeter of rectangle AEFG?	

4. 6 Min.	If <u>a</u> is divided by <u>b</u>, the result is 3/4. If <u>b</u> is divided by <u>c</u>, the result is 5/6.
	What is the result when <u>a</u> *is divided by* <u>c</u>?

5. 6 Min.	Find the greatest number that divides 364, 414, and 539 with the same remainder in each case.

1.
3 Min.
In the XYZ contest, a school may enter 1, 2, 3, or, at most, 4 teams. If 347 teams are entered in the XYZ contest,

What is the smallest number of schools that could have entered the XYZ contest?

2.
4 Min.
What is the total of:
one plus two plus three plus four plus five plus six plus
one plus two plus three plus four plus five plus six plus
one plus two plus three plus four plus five plus six plus
one plus two plus three plus four plus five plus six plus
one plus two plus three plus four plus five?

3.
5 Min.

$$\frac{1}{2 + \frac{1}{2}} \quad + \quad \frac{1}{3 + \frac{1}{3}}$$

Express the above as a simple fraction in lowest terms.

4.
5 Min.
Alice started a Math Club during the first week of school. As the only member, she decided to recruit two new members during the following week of school. Each new member, during the week following the week when he or she became a member, recruits two new members.

How many members will the club have at the end of five weeks?

5.
6 Min.
One light flashes every 2 minutes and another light flashes every 3½ minutes. Suppose both lights flash together at noon.

What is the first time after 1 P.M. that both lights will flash together?

1. **4 Min.**	In the subtraction problem at the right, each letter represents a digit, and different letters represent different digits.

$$\begin{array}{r} A\ B\ A \\ -\ \ C\ A \\ \hline A\ B \end{array}$$

What digit does C represent?

---

2. **4 Min.**	Each of the small boxes in the figure at the right is a square. The perimeter of square ABCD is 36 cm.

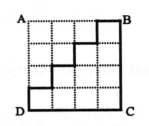

What is the perimeter of the figure shown with darkened outline?

---

3. **5 Min.**	2^3 means 2 x 2 x 2 or 8. 3^3 means 3 x 3 x 3 or 27. N^3 means N x N x N. Suppose $N^3 = 4,913$.

What is the value of N?

---

4. **6 Min.**	Carl shot 3 arrows; 2 landed in the A ring and 1 landed in circle B for a total score of 17. David also shot 3 arrows; 1 landed in A and 2 in B for a total score of 22.

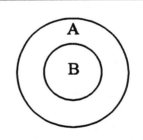

How many points are assigned to circle B?

---

5. **5 Min.**	In the following sequence of numbers, each number has one more 1 than the preceding number: 1, 11, 111, 1111, 11111, . . .

What is the tens digit of the sum of the first 30 numbers of the sequence?

1.
4 Min.
There are 4 separate large boxes, and inside each large box there are 3 separate small boxes, and inside each of these small boxes there are 2 separate smaller boxes.

How many boxes, counting all sizes, are there altogether?

2.
6 Min.
When asked how many gold coins he had, the collector said:
    If I arrange them in stacks of five, none are left over.
    If I arrange them in stacks of six, none are left over.
    If I arrange them in stacks of seven, one is left over.

What is the least number of coins he could have?

3.
6 Min.
The length of the shortest trip from A to B along the edges of the cube shown is the length of 3 edges.

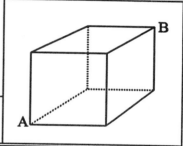

How many different 3-edge trips are there from A to B?

4.
5 Min.
How many two-digit numbers are there in which the tens digit is greater than the ones digit?

5.
6 Min.
Alice and Betty run a 50-meter race and Alice wins by 10 meters. They then run a 60-meter race, and each girl runs at the same speed she ran in the first race.

By how many meters will Alice win?

1. **4 Min.**	At the right, the sum of two 3-digit numbers is represented. A, B, and C represent the digits 2, 3 and 5 but not necessarily in the same order, and different letters represent different digits.

B A C
+ C A B
‾‾‾‾‾‾‾

What is the largest value the indicated sum could have?

---

2. **5 Min.**	$(5273)^2$ means 5273 x 5273; $(5273)^3$ means 5273 x 5273 x 5273; and so forth. When $(5273)^6$ is completely multiplied out,

what will the units (or ones) digit be in the resulting product?

---

3. **5 Min.**	A baseball league has nine teams. During the season, each of the nine teams plays exactly three games with each of the other teams.

What is the total number of games played?

---

4. **6 Min.**	June has 30 days. One year, June had exactly four Sundays.

On which two days of the week could June 30 not have occurred that year?

---

5. **6 Min.**	The six faces of a three-inch wooden cube are each painted red. The cube is then cut into one-inch cubes along the lines shown in the diagram.

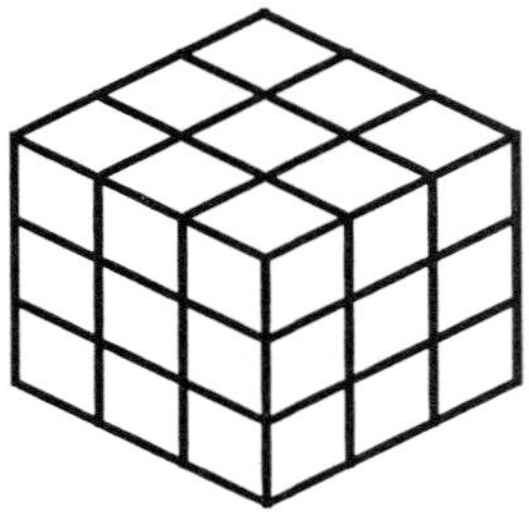

How many of the one-inch cubes have red paint on at least two faces?

1.
4 Min.
The serial number of my camera is a four-digit number less than 5,000 and contains the digits 2, 3, 5, and 8 but not necessarily in that order. The "3" is next to the "8", the "2" is not next to the "3", and the "5" is not next to the "2".

What is the serial number?

2.
5 Min.
One day, Carol bought apples at 3 for 25¢ and sold all of them at 2 for 25¢.

If she made a profit of $1, how many apples did she sell that day?

3.
5 Min.
As shown, ABCD and AFED are squares with a common side AD of length 10 cm. Arc BD and arc DF are quarter-circles.

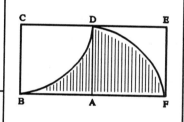

How many square cm. are in the area of the shaded region?

4.
6 Min.
When the same whole number is added to both the numerator and denominator of 2/5, the value of the new fraction is 2/3.

What was the number added to both the numerator and denominator?

5.
6 Min.
The sum of the ages of three children is 32. The age of the oldest is twice the age of the youngest. The ages of the two older children differ by three years.

What is the age of the youngest child?

1.
4 Min.

A slow clock loses 3 minutes every hour. Suppose the slow clock and a correct clock both show the correct time at 9 A.M.

What time will the slow clock show when the correct clock shows 10 o'clock the evening of the same day?

2.
5 Min.

The figure at the right is a "magic square" with missing entries. When complete, the sum of the four entries in each column, each row, and each diagonal is the same.

A		7	12
	4	9	
	5	16	
8	11		B

Find the value of A and the value of B.

3.
5 Min.

The digit 3 is written at the right of a certain two-digit number thus forming a three-digit number. The new number is 372 more than the original two-digit number.

What was the original two-digit number?

4.
6 Min.

ABCD is a square with area 16 sq. meters. E and F are midpoints of sides AB and BC, respectively.

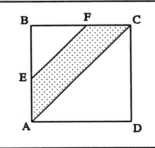

What is the area of trapezoid AEFC, the shaded region?

5.
6 Min.

Peter agreed to work after school for 8 weeks at a fixed weekly rate. But instead of being given only money, he was to be given $85 and a bicycle. However, Peter worked only 5 weeks at the fixed weekly rate and was given $25 and the bicycle.

How much was the bicycle worth?

1.
3 Min.
Suppose the time is now 2 o'clock on a twelve-hour clock which runs continuously.

What time will it show 1,000 hours from now?

2.
4 Min.
The average of five numbers is 6. If one of the five numbers is removed, the average of the four remaining numbers is 7.

What is the value of the number that was removed?

3.
5 Min.
If you start with 3 and count by 7s, you get the terms of the sequence 3, 10, 17, . . . , 528 where 3 is the 1st term, 10 is the 2nd term, 17 is the 3rd term, and so forth up to 528 which is the Nth term.

What is the value of N?

4.
5 Min.
When a natural number is multiplied by itself, the result is a perfect square. For example 1, 4, and 9 are perfect squares because 1x1 = 1, 2x2 = 4, and 3x3 = 9.

How many perfect squares are less than 10,000?

5.
5 Min.
A restaurant has a total of 30 tables which are of two types. The first type seats two people at each table; the second type seats five people at each table. A total of 81 people are seated when all seats are occupied.

How many tables for two are there?

1. **4 Min.**	The cost of a book is $1 and a whole number of cents. The total cost of six copies of the book is less than $8. However, the total cost of seven copies of the same book at the same price per book is more than $8.

What is the least a single copy of the book could cost?

2. **5 Min.**	The sum of all digits in the numbers 34, 35, and 36 is 24 because $(3+4) + (3+5) + (3+6) = 24$.

Find the sum of all digits in the first twenty-five natural numbers:
1, 2, 3, 4, 5, . . . , 23, 24, 25

3. **5 Min.**	Alice earned a total of $65 for working five days after school. Each day after the first day, she earned $2 more than she earned the day before.

How much did she earn on the first day?

4. **5 Min.**	Each of the small boxes in the figure at the right is a square and the area of the figure is 52 square units,

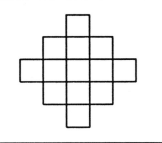

How many units are there in the outer perimeter of the figure?

5. **5 Min.**	A work team of four people completes half of a job in 15 days.

How many days will it take a team of ten people to complete the remaining half of the job? (Assume that each person of both teams works at the same rate as each of the other people.)

Olympiad 43

1.
2 Min.

Two cash registers of a store had a combined total of $300. When the manager transferred $15 from one register to the other register, each register then had the same amount.

How much did the register with the larger amount have before the transfer was made?

2.
4 Min.

The product of two numbers is 128 and their quotient is 8.

What are the numbers?

3.
6 Min.

In the figure at the right, each number represents the length of the segment which is nearest it.

How many square units are in the area of the figure if there is a right angle at each corner of the figure?

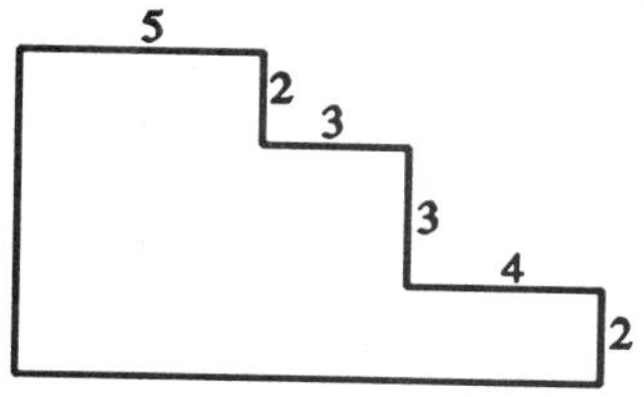

4.
5 Min.

In the addition problem at the right, different letters stand for different digits. AH represents a two-digit number and HEE represents a three-digit number.

What number does HEE represent?

$$\begin{array}{r} A\ H \\ +\ A \\ \hline H\ E\ E \end{array}$$

5.
6 Min.

Barbara has 20 coins consisting of nickels and dimes. If the nickels were dimes and the dimes were nickels, she would have 30¢ more than she has now.

How many dimes did she have to begin with?

1.
4 Min. I am less than 6 feet tall but more than 2 feet tall. My height in inches is a multiple of 7 and is also 2 inches more than a multiple of 6.

What is my height in inches?

2.
5 Min. In the multiplication example at the right, A and B represent different digits, AB is a two-digit number and BBB is a three-digit number. (* means multiply.)

$$\begin{array}{r} A\ B \\ *\ 6 \\ \hline B\ B\ B \end{array}$$

What two-digit number does AB represent?

3.
5 Min. Tom went to a store and spent one-third of his money. He went to a second store where he spent one-third of what remained, and then had $12 when he left.

How much money did he have to begin with at the first store?

4.
6 Min. The tower at the right has no gaps. Suppose it is painted red on all exterior sides including the bottom, and then cut into cubes along the indicated lines.

How many cubes will each have red paint on just three faces?

5.
6 Min. A9543B represents a six-digit number in which A and B are digits different from each other.

If the number is divisible by 11 and also by 8, what digit does A represent?

1. **4 Min.**	In Nogatco, a primitive country, "OC" means a bundle of 8 sticks, "OCTA" means a bundle of 8 OCs, "OCTIL" means a bundle of 8 OCTAs, and "OCTILLA" means a bundle of 8 OCTILs.
	How many sticks are in an OCTILLA?

2. **5 Min.**	When certain numbers are placed in the empty boxes, the sum of the three numbers in each of the three rows, three columns, and two diagonals is the same.	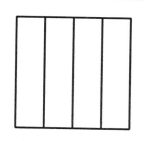
	What number should be in the center box?	

3. **6 Min.**	In basketball, a field goal is worth 2 points and a foul shot is worth 1 point. Suppose a team scored 72 points and made 6 more field goals than foul shots,
	How many foul shots did the team make?

4. **5 Min.**	The square at the right is divided into four congruent rectangles. The perimeter of each of the four congruent rectangles is 25 units.	
	How many units are there in the perimeter of the square?	

5. **6 Min.**	1^2 means 1x1, 2^2 means 2x2, 3^2 means 3x3, and so forth. If $1^2 + 2^2 + 3^2 + 4^2 + \ldots + 25^2 = 5525$, and if $2^2 + 4^2 + 6^2 + 8^2 + \ldots + 50^2 = N$,
	find the value of N.

1.
3 Min.

A purse contains 4 pennies, 2 nickels, 1 dime, and 1 quarter. Different values can be obtained by using one or more coins in the purse.

How many different values can be obtained?

2.
5 Min.

Tickets for a concert cost $2 each for children and $5 each for adults. A group of thirty people consisting of children and adults paid a total of $87 for the concert.

How many adults were in the group?

3.
6 Min.

The tower shown at the right is made of horizontal layers of unit cubes, not all being visible in the diagram.

How many unit cubes are contained in the tower?

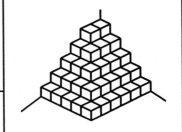

4.
5 Min.

The average of five numbers is 16. Suppose 10 is added to the five numbers.

What is the average of the six numbers?

5.
6 Min.

For the division problem at right:
A, B, and C are different digits,
each of AB and 7C is a 2-digit number, and
each blank space represents a missing digit.

What is the value of each of A, B, and C?

```
          7 C
A B / _ _ _ _
      _ _
      ─────
      _ _ _
      _ 2 _
      ─────
        0
```

1.
4 Min.
A certain brand of sardines is usually sold at 3 cans for $2. Suppose the price is changed to 4 cans for $2.50.

Will the new cost for 12 cans be more or less than the usual cost for 12 cans, and by how much?

2.
5 Min.
N is the number of buttons in a sewing box.
  a. N is more than 40 but less than 80.
  b. When N is divided by 5, the remainder is 2.
  c. When N is divided by 7, the remainder is 4.

Find the value of N.

3.
5 Min.
Consecutive numbers are whole numbers that follow in order such as 3, 4, 5.

Find the smallest of the five consecutive numbers whose sum is 100.

4.
5 Min.
A dog takes 3 steps to walk the same distance for which a cat takes 4 steps. Suppose 1 step of the dog covers 1 foot.

How many feet would the cat cover in taking 12 steps?

5.
6 Min.
In the addition problem at the right, different letters represent different digits. It is also given that N is 6 and T is greater than 1.

```
  T H I S
  +   I S
  -------
  K E E N
```

What four-digit number does T H I S represent? (Be sure to write your answer as a four-digit number.)

1. 5 Min.	(1,1,8) is a triple of natural numbers which has a sum of 10.

How many different triples of natural numbers have a sum of 10 if the order of the three numbers in the triple does not matter? Include (1,1,8) as one of your triples. (Note that (1,1,8), (1,8,1) and (8,1,1) are considered to be the same triple.)

2. 5 Min.	Patricia has $12 more than Rhoda and $15 more than Sarah. Together all three have $87.

How much does Patricia have?

3. 6 Min.	The "staircase" at the right is 4 units tall and contains 10 unit squares. Suppose the staircase were extended until it was 12 units tall.	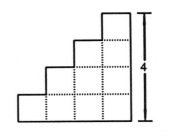

How many unit squares would it then contain all together?

4. 6 Min.	If I start with the number 7 and count by 4's, the following sequence is obtained: 7, 11, 15, 19, 23, and so forth. A new sequence is formed when I start with a different number and count by a different number. Suppose the 2nd number of the new sequence is 8 and the 5th number is 17.

What is the 10th number of the new sequence?

5. 5 Min.	The entire treasury of the Alpha club, consisting of $240, was to be divided into equal shares for each club member. When it was discovered that one member was not eligible for a share, the share of each of the remaining members increased by $1.

How many eligible members got a share of the $240?

1.
4 Min.

There are many three-digit numbers that are each divisible by 7 and also by 8 without remainder in each case.

What is the largest of these three-digit numbers?

2.
5 Min.

Twenty-four meters of fencing is used to fence a rectangular garden. Let M represents the number of square meters in the area of the garden.

What is the largest value that M could have?

3.
6 Min.

When a certain number N is divided by 3, the result is the same as when N is decreased by 8.

What is the number N?

4.
5 Min.

A package weighs P pounds, P being a whole number. To ship this package by express costs $1.65 for the first five pounds and 12¢ for each additional pound. The total shipping cost was $3.45.

How many pounds did the package weigh?

5.
5 Min.

The sum $\frac{1}{2} + \frac{.1}{2} + \frac{1}{.2}$ is equal to the decimal A.BC where A, B, and C may be the same or different digits.

What number does A.BC represent?

| 1.
5 Min. | In the U.S.A., the symbol 5/2 means the 5th month, 2nd day, or May 2. But in England, 5/2 means the fifth day, 2nd month, or February 5. |

How many days of the year each have the same symbol in both the U.S.A. and England?

| 2.
4 Min. | The product of two numbers is 504 and each of the numbers is divisible by 6. However, neither of the two numbers is 6. |

What is the larger of the two numbers?

| 3.
6 Min. | A rectangular garden is 14 ft. by 21 ft. and is bordered by a concrete walk 3 ft. wide as shown. |

Walk

Garden

Walk

How many square feet are in the surface area of just the concrete walk?

| 4.
6 Min. | Four numbers are arranged in order of size and the difference between any two adjacent numbers is the same. Suppose 1/3 is the first and 1/2 is the fourth of these numbers. |

What are the two numbers between 1/3 and 1/2?

| 5.
7 Min. | Each of the three diagrams at the right shows a balance of weights using different objects. |

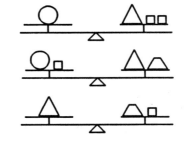

How many □s will balance a ◯ ?

Answers

Olympiad 1
1) Thursday
2) 19
3) 325
4) 12¢
5) 15 days

Olympiad 2
1) made $10
2) 17 nickels, 13 quarters
3) 144
4) 154
5) 200

Olympiad 3
1) 60
2) 24 or 24 mph
3) A = 7
4) 5/6
5) 298

Olympiad 4
1) $140
2) A=3, B=8
3) 11
4) A=4, B=12
5) 5

Olympiad 5
1) 60
2) 10 min.
3) 12/29
4) 15, 21, 35
5) 15 small, 2 large

Olympiad 6
1) 99
2) 78
3) 12 or 12 g
4) 5p, 13n, 3d; or 10p, 4n, 7d
5) 13

Olympiad 7
1) 6666
2) 9
3) F
4) 8 days
5) 96

Olympiad 8
1) 21
2) 12
3) 38
4) $36
5) 4

Olympiad 9
1) 20
2) 150
3) 5
4) 140 min or 2 hr 20 min
5) A=3, B=8

Olympiad 10
1) H=2, E=3, A=9
2) 26
3) A=3, B=2
4) 22
5) 3

Olympiad 11
1) IV, II, I, V, III
2) 15,762
3) Glenn-tennis, Harry-Soccer, Kim-baseball
4) 10
5) 7

Olympiad 12
1) 312132 or 231213
2) Friday
3) 6
4) 4d, 12n
5) 57

Olympiad 13
1) 22
2) 625 or 875
3) 58, 59, 60
4) Anne; $2
5) 6

Olympiad 14
1) 5
2) 7
3) D
4) 4, or 4 hr
5) 15

Olympiad 15
1) 12
2) 8
3) $30
4) 32
5) 7

Olympiad 16
1) Tuesday
2) 54
3) 5
4) E, A, N
5) D is greater; 50

Olympiad 17
1) 5p, 2d
2) 90¢ or $.90
3) 60 or 60 in.
4) 23
5) 9

Olympiad 18
1) 86 or 86 lb.
2) 42, 43
3) 4
4) 26
5) 10

Olympiad 19
1) 5 or $5
2) A=4, B=7, C=5
3) M=12
4) $60
5) A=5, B=6

Olympiad 20
1) 45 or 45 mi.
2) 91
3) 29 in.
4) 10 or 10 min
5) 24 or 24¢

Olympiad 21
1) 40
2) 15
3) $350 or 350
4) 8
5) $150 or 150

Olympiad 22
1) Wednesday
2) 19
3) 96
4) 26
5) 13

Olympiad 23
1) 21
2) 48
3) 13
4) 14
5) 1.5 or 1½

Olympiad 24
1) 1976
2) 24
3) 10
4) 16 & 625, or 2^4 & 5^4
5) 1/10 mi. or 528 ft.

Olympiad 25
1) 55
2) 45
3) 24, 25, 26
4) $2\frac{1}{6}$ or 13/6
5) 8

Olympiad 26
1) Thursday
2) 120
3) 6
4) 6 or 6 days
5) 11, 15, 33, 55

Olympiad 27
1) 7
2) 20
3) A=9, B=1, C=8
4) 1936
5) 94

Olympiad 28
I) 1,560
2) 720
3) 60
4) 16
5) 20

Olympiad 29
1) 72
2) 9
3) 17
4) 7
5) 342

Olympiad 30
1) 198
2) 5
3) 440
4) A=7, B=8, C=3; or 7, 8, 3
5) 15 or 15¢

Olympiad 31
1) 6
2) 35
3) 90
4) 720
5) 1009

Olympiad 32
1) 8
2) 45
3) Bill, 18
4) 24
5) 15

Olympiad 33
1) 8 or 8 oz.
2) 71
3) 35
4) 10:20 or 10:20 A.M.
5) 5

Olympiad 34
1) 950
2) 95¢ or equivalent
3) 30 or 30 m
4) 5/8
5) 25

Olympiad 35
1) 87
2) 99
3) 7/10
4) 31
5) 1:10

Olympiad 36
1) 9
2) 36 or 36 cm
3) 17
4) 9
5) 2

Olympiad 37
1) 40
2) 120
3) 6
4) 45
5) 12 or 12 m

Olympiad 38
1) 848
2) 9
3) 108
4) Sun, Mon
5) 20

Olympiad 39
1) 2835
2) 24
3) 100 or 100 sq cm
4) 4
5) 7

Olympiad 40
1) 9:21 or 21:21
2) A=1, B=13
3) 41
4) 6
5) $75 or 75

Olympiad 41
1) 6 o'clock
2) 2
3) 76
4) 99
5) 23

Olympiad 42
1) $1.15 or 115¢
2) 127
3) $9 or 9
4) 40
5) 6

Olympiad 43
1) $165
2) 4 and 32
3) 58
4) 100
5) 7

Olympiad 44
1) 56
2) 74
3) 27 or $27
4) 11
5) A=7

Olympiad 45
1) 4096
2) 11
3) 20
4) 40
5) 22,100

Olympiad 46
1) 49
2) 9
3) 70
4) 15
5) A=1, B=4, C=9

Olympiad 47
1) $.50 or 50¢ less
2) 67
3) 18
4) 9
5) 7953

Olympiad 48
1) 8
2) $38 or 38
3) 78
4) 32
5) 15

Olympiad 49
1) 952
2) 36
3) 12
4) 20 or 20 lb
5) 5.55

Olympiad 50
1) 12
2) 42
3) 246, or 246 sq ft
4) 7/18 and 8/18, or equivalent
5) 6

Hints

Olympiad 1

1) What day will it be 7 days from now? 14 days from now?

2) Make an organized list of the different amounts that can be made starting with the 3¢-stamps.

3) Rewrite the series in reverse order placing each term directly under each term of the given series. Examine each vertical pair.

4) How much will 5 pens and 5 pencils cost?

5) How long would it take one person to do the entire job alone?

Olympiad 2

1) Act it out.

2) Try using half of the coins as nickels and the other half as quarters.

3) How many square inches are there in the rectangular sheet 2 feet by 3 feet?

4) If the average score for four games is 145, what is the total score for the games?

5) If you counted from 1 on, how frequently would "1" appear in the units place? tens place? hundreds place?

Olympiad 3

1) Try a simpler problem. Suppose there were just 2 or 3 children.

2) Average speed is the total distance divided by the total time.

3) If a number is divisible by 9, the sum of its digits is also divisible by 9.

4) $\dfrac{1}{9 \times 10} = \dfrac{1}{9} - \dfrac{1}{10}$

5) Compare the terms of the sequence with the multiples of 3.

Olympiad 4

1) Make both 1.75 and 1¼ either decimal numbers or mixed numbers.

2) A x AB = 114. Try different values for A starting with 2.

3) Experiment.

4) Could A be less than 3?

5) Do (6*8) first.

Olympiad 5

1) What is the average of the five numbers?

2) How many times bigger than 600 sq feet is 600 sq yards?

3) Work backward.

4) What is the largest number that the two-digit numbers can divide without remainder?

5) Try packaging some marbles in the larger boxes and examine what is left over.

Olympiad 6

1) Make X + Y as large as possible and X – Y as small as possible.

2) Arrange the numbers to be summed like so:

$$\begin{array}{cccccc} 1 & 2 & 3 & 4 & 5 & 6 \\ 12 & 11 & 10 & 9 & 8 & 7 \end{array}$$

Examine each of the vertical pairs. What do you notice?

3) What is the total weight of the original group of five weights?

4) Could you have as many as 15 pennies? What is the least number of pennies you could have?

5) Make a Venn diagram which shows the relationship between students who take French and those who take Spanish.

Olympiad 7

1) Follow the directions carefully.

2) Make a list of the different pairs of coins. Try to arrange the pairs in numerical order starting with (1,1) as the first pair.

3) Divide each of the numbers in column A by 7. What do you observe?

4) If all the supplies were used for just one person, how long would the supplies last?

5) What is the area of each square? What is the length of a side of the square?

Olympiad 8

1) How many beads must I pick blindfolded before I can be sure that I have a pair of the same color?

2) How many thirds are there in 2?

3) Count the squares in an orderly fashion starting with 1 by 1 squares, then 2 by 2 squares, and so forth.

4) Work backward.

5) What prime factors must a number have so that it ends in one zero?

Olympiad 9

1) What should the sum of the numbers in each row, column, and diagonal be?

2) What is the difference between each pair of successive numbers? Compare the numbers with the multiples of 3.

3) List the possible dimensions in some orderly manner.

4) How do you determine the number of hours a trip will take if you know the distance and the rate of speed of the car?

5) The product of 5_ and B is 432. What number do you think B should be? Can you now tell what is the units digit of the divisor?

Olympiad 10

1) Can H = 3? What is the largest value that H might have? The smallest value?

2) List pairs of numbers whose product is 144.

3) Change B/3 to an equivalent fraction with denominator 33. What is the largest value B could have?

4) Can 121 be factored?

5) Suppose the student passed 7 tests and failed 1. How much would he receive?

Olympiad 11

1) Follow the directions carefully.

2) What units digit in the top line multiplied by 7 will yield the 2 in the first partial product? What tens digit in the top line will yield the 8 in the first partial product?

3) Make a table showing the names of individuals G,H,K, and sports t,b,s. Enter Y in the table if the individual likes the sport and N if he does not like the sport.

	SPORTS		
	t	b	s
G			
H			
K			

4) Mark the different rays by a, b, c, d, e. List the pairs of rays that form different angles starting with the smallest angles.

5) In the first condition, replace 1 pear by 4 plums and 1 apple.

Olympiad 12

1) Draw 6 blanks: __ __ __ __ __ __ . Place the digits in the spaces according to the given directions. Begin with the digit 3.

2) Mark a line diagram Y, T, and W to represent yesterday, today, and tomorrow, respectively.

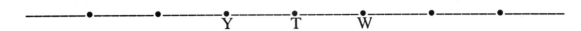

Now find the points in the line referred to in the given information.

3) Draw a diagram for each path. Start by going to the right as far as possible and then up. Follow the same procedure in the next path without duplicating the previous path.

4) Suppose all the coins were nickels. By how much would it be short of a dollar? How many nickels should be replaced by dimes?

5) How does the remainder compare with each divisor? What would you add to the number being divided so that there would be a zero remainder?

Olympiad 13

1) What size squares can be found in the figure? How many of each size are there?

2) The product C x C has a units digit C. There are 4 digits which satisfy this condition and two of them are 0 and 1. But 0 and 1 will not satisfy other conditions. What are the other two digits?

3) You know the sum of the first and third numbers. Can you tell what the second number is?

4) If you add the different given amounts of money, what will the sum represent?

5) Try making the three smaller piles as large as possible.

Olympiad 14

1) What is the semiperimeter of the rectangle? What pairs of dimensions will yield the semiperimeter?

2) How many points would Nancy have if all her answers were correct? How many points less than a perfect score was her actual score?

3) Continue the entries into the table until you reach 24. Examine the remainders when the numbers in each column are divided by 8.

4) What part of the pool will the first pipe fill in 1 hour? the second pipe? the third pipe? Together, what part will they fill in 1 hour?

5) Find the sum that each column, row, and diagonal should have.

Olympiad 15

1) What is the sum of the first five numbers? the next five? How much more is needed to make a sum of 78?

2) In the diagram at the right, an outer vertical slice has been removed. Each cube of this slice has paint on one or more faces. How many cubes in the second slice will not have paint on any face?

Outer Slice   Second Slice

3) What is the smallest purchase that can be paid for either by two-dollar bills or by five-dollar bills? Compare the number of two-dollar bills with the number of five-dollar bills used for the smallest purchase.

4) How many gallons does 1/4 of the tank hold?

5) Look for a pattern in the units-digit of multiplication strings.

Olympiad 16

1) What day of the month was the Friday before the 25th of the month? two Fridays before the 25th of the month?

2) If AB represents the man's age, then the addition at the right is given. What is the sum of the digits of the man's age?

$$\begin{array}{r} A\,B \\ +\,B\,A \\ \hline 9\,9 \end{array}$$

3) How many buggies were used in going to the fair?

4) Which letters cannot be opposite H?

5) How many numbers in the D-sum? N-sum? Remove "1" from the D-sum. Now compare each number of the D-sum with each number of the N-sum.

Olympiad 17

1) Could each of the remaining coins be nickels?

2) Suppose the second purchase was cut in half. Compare this with the first purchase.

3) How many sides of the unit squares are contained in the perimeter of A?

4) The number of children is 3 more than a multiple of 4. List the first six numbers that satisfy this condition. The number of children is also 2 less than a multiple of 5. List the first six numbers that satisfy this condition.

5) What is A + C? What must A be?

Olympiad 18

1) What is the average weight of Tom and Bill? How much more than the average does the heavier boy weigh?

2) Could the two page numbers be in the 50's? the 40's? What could the units digits be?

3) Place a dot on each cube that has exactly 4 red faces.

4) 169 can be factored. Find its factors.

5) What is the middle number of the 15 consecutive numbers?

Olympiad 19

1) What is the average cost of the camera and case? How much more than the average cost is the camera?

2) Find B in the second addition.

3) From the first two sums of 11 and 19, how much more than K is M? Since M + K = 16, can you now find M?

4) Work backward.

5) The six-digit number is also divisible by 8 and 9.

Olympiad 20

1) How many seconds in 1 min 20 sec? in 1 hour?

2) If the number is divided by 15, what will the remainder be? List the numbers less than 100 which have a remainder of 1 when divided by 15.

3) Check the given lengths. Can 29 be represented as a sum of 6's and 7's?

4) Where is each cyclist after 10 minutes?

5) What is the least the ruler could cost? Fill in the following table for different costs of the ruler:

cost of ruler	am't Alice has	am't Betty has	am't together

Olympiad 21

1) What is the the total value of one nickel and one dime in cents?

2) Can A = 0? Notice that the product 7 x A ends in A. What digit must A be?

3) Express 1¾ as decimal number.

4) Place a dot on each cube that has 2 or 4 red faces. Why can't one of the blocks have 6 red faces?

5) What is the average amount received by the 4 brothers? How much more than the youngest does the oldest get? Then how much less than the average does the youngest get?

Olympiad 22

1) What day of the week is today? What day of the week will it be 7 days from today? 14 days from today?

2) Work backward.

3) How many sq. in. are there in the square region?

4) If each arrow lands on the target, what is the smallest score possible? largest score possible?

5) Try the same problem with simple numbers, say 5 and 8. Does your answer seem to have a connection with the numbers 5 and 8? Try it with 7 and 11.

Olympiad 23

1) What is the sum of the five numbers before each is increased?

2) Count the cubes in one slice.

3) What is the smallest square greater than 1,000? largest square less than 2,000? Express both squares in the form: N^2.

4) Suppose each tricycle is placed with its two rear wheels on the ground and the front wheel up off the ground, and each bicycle has its two wheels on the ground. How many wheels are on the ground all together? How many wheels are off the ground?

5) What was the weight of the water poured out? What was the weight of the water remaining in the jar?

Olympiad 24

1) How old is person A when person B is born?

2) How many sides of the square are equivalent to the 18 in. perimeter of the rectangle?

3) AB x A yields the second partial product. Then AB x A ends in 1. What digits must A and B be?

4) 10 = 2x5;   10x10 = 100 = 2x5x2x5 or 2x2x5x5 or 4x25.

5) Make a diagram of the tunnel and the train as the train is about to enter the tunnel. Now show the train on the same diagram when the train clears the tunnel. How many train-lengths did the train travel from the time it entered the tunnel to the time it cleared the tunnel?

Olympiad 25

1) To satisfy the condition of divisibility by 5 as stated, what must the multiple of 7 end in?

2) Represent the people by A, B, C, D, E, and F. Let any pair of letters represent a match. Make a listing of the different matches played in one round. See the *Solutions* section for another interesting method, p. 143.

3) 10x10x10 = 1,000; 20x20x20 = ?; 30x30x30 = ? Supply the information requested above. Between what two multiples of 10 are the three consecutive numbers located? For the product to have two terminal zeros, what must one of the three consecutive numbers be?

4) If the average of all three numbers is 1, what must their sum be?

5) If a number is divisible by 36, it is also divisible by 9 and by 4. What digits can B be? If a number is divisible by 9, the sum of its digits is a multiple of 9. (Show that A + B cannot equal 17.)

Olympiad 26

1) How many days are there from Jan 1 to Feb 22? On what day-numbers will Mondays occur?

2) If all the X's of the large rectangle were shown, how many would there be? How many X's are missing?

3) (1,1,24) is one of the triples whose product is 24. Find the other triples. (It will be easier to list them if you write the numbers in each triple in increasing order.) Remember to count (1,1,24) as one of the triples.

4) How long would the food last if it was used by just one scout?

5) What is the largest number that each of the two-digit numbers will divide with no remainder?

Olympiad 27

1) Think of the possible values of the 13¢-stamps that were purchased. What should the units digit be?

2) What is the length of a side of the square?

3) Examine the units column. What is A+B? Now examine the tens column. Remember the carry of 1 from the units column. What is B+C? What is B?

4) 30x30 = ?   40x40 = ?   50x50 = ?
Which four-digit square number begins with 19__?

5) Let TU be the largest two-digit number satisfying the condition shown at the right. What is the largest value that T could have? Now find U.

$$\begin{array}{r} T\,U \\ -U\,T \\ \hline 4\ 5 \end{array}$$

Olympiad 28

1) What is the largest value that A x B could have? Do your values for A and B also give the smallest value that A – B could have?

2) How many minutes must the slow clock lose before it again shows the correct time?

3) If a number is divisible by 3 and also by 5, the number must be a multiple of 15. List some multiples of 15 and check each against the other condition of the problem.

4) Place a dot on each cube which has exactly 3 red faces. Start with the bottom layer.

5) What part of the job will Alice do in one minute? Betty in one minute? together in one minute?

Olympiad 29

1) Find the smallest and largest multiples of 3 between 10 and 226. Express these multiples in the form 3 x N.

2) Divide the rectangle into triangles which are each congruent to triangle BEF.

3) Express 85 as the product of two factors neither of which is 1. Which of the two factors is the sum of the two whole numbers?

4) Did you remember that 25 is 5 x 5 in factored form?

5) How many pages require 1 piece of type each? 2 pieces of type each? 3 pieces of type each?

Olympiad 30

1) How frequently do 2 or 7 appear as the units digit of a number in the sequence of natural numbers?

2) When four coins are taken out of the pocket, how many are left in the pocket?

3) How many complete turns will the front wheel make in travelling 1 mile? the rear wheel?

4) What values could C have? Try one. Now find B and then A. Will these values work when they are substituted for the letters? If not, find another value for C.

5) Work backward.

Hints

Olympiad 31

1) What fractional part of the weight of the whole brick was 4 pounds?

2) What is the middle number of the 7 consecutive numbers?

3) List the numbers between 100 and 200 that have the required property. Now determine how many other numbers have the required property.

4) How far will the wheel roll on the ground in making one complete turn?

5) What is the value of D? E? R?

Olympiad 32

1) What was the number that Tom multiplied 2½ by to get 50?

2) Answer the following questions to determine between what two multiples of 10 the number is located.
$$30 \times 30 = ? \quad 40 \times 40 = ? \quad 50 \times 50 = ? \quad 60 \times 60 = ?$$

3) What does the sum 25 + 20 + 31 represent?

4) What is the total perimeter of the three rectangles in terms of a side s of the square?

5) What is the largest amount that can be made from the four coins? Can all amounts from 1 through the largest amount be made with the four coins?

Olympiad 33

1) What is the weight of the marbles that were added to the bowl and its original marbles?

2) Suppose you have found the smallest odd number which when divided by 5 or 7 has a remainder of 1. What will happen when that number is divided by 35?

3) Find the number of cubes in the tallest column. Can you find the number of cubes in each of the other columns?

4) When the correct clock moves 60 minutes, how many minutes does the slow clock move? When the correct clock moves 4 minutes, how many minutes does the slow clock move?

5) Work backward.

Olympiad 34

1) What is the average of the first 25 natural numbers? What is the average of the next 25 natural numbers?

2) Suppose Eric has just 1 nickel. How does that affect the number of quarters and the number of dimes?

3) What is the length of a side of square ABCD?

4) What does $\frac{a}{b} \times \frac{b}{c}$ equal?

5) See hint for Olympiad 22 problem 5.

Olympiad 35

1) What is the largest number of schools that can enter four teams in the XYZ contest?

2) Find the sum of the numbers in the first line.

3) Express each denominator as an improper fraction.

4) Make a table showing the number of new members in each of the five weeks.

5) How frequently do both lights flash together?

Olympiad 36

1) What value does A have? B? C?

2) How many "vertical risers" does the staircase have? How many "horizontal treads" does the staircase have? What total length do the four risers have?

3) Use the following questions to determine between what multiples of 10 the number N must lie.

$$10 \times 10 \times 10 = ? \qquad 20 \times 20 \times 20 = ? \qquad 30 \times 30 \times 30 = ?$$

What units digit for N will produce the units digit of 4913?

4) What does the sum of Carl's and David's scores represent in terms of arrows on the target? What is the total point value of 1 arrow in the A-ring and 1 arrow in the B-ring?

5) How many 1's are in the units column of the first 30 numbers?

Olympiad 37

1) Count the "large" boxes, the "small" boxes, and the "smaller" boxes in that order.

2) If the coins are arranged in stacks of 30, would any be left over?

3) Make a diagram of each path

4) Consider the set 00, 01, 02, . . . , 99. How many numbers are in the set? How many numbers have the same digit in the tens and units places? How many numbers have different digits in the tens and units places?

5) When Alice runs 50m, how many m does Betty run? When Alice runs 5m, how many m does Betty run?

Olympiad 38

1) Experiment.

2) What in the given four-digit number determines the units digit of the product?

3) Solve a simpler problem. Suppose each team played just one game with each of the other teams. See *Solutions,* Olympiad 25, problem 2, method 2.

4) Could Sunday occur on the first day of the month? on the second day of the month?

5) How many cubes are there all together? How many do not have paint on any face? How many have paint on just one face?

Olympiad 39

1) Use this diagram _ _ _ _ to enter the numbers. If there is more than one possible arrangement, show it in another diagram.

2) What is a convenient number of apples to buy and sell with none left over?

3) Compare the shaded regions with the unshaded regions.

4) Test adding the same whole number to the numerator and denominator of 2/5. Start with 1: (2+1)/(5+1) = 3/6 or 1/2.

5) Make a table of the ages with 5 as the youngest.

Age of youngest	Age of next older	Age of oldest	Sum of ages
5			

Olympiad 40

1) How many hours elapsed from 9AM to 10PM? How many minutes did the slow clock lose?

2) What should the sum of the numbers in each row, column, and diagonal be?

3) Suppose the original two-digit number is TU. Now express the other conditions of the problem using TU.

4) Divide the entire region into triangles congruent to triangle EBF.

5) How much did Peter lose in dollars by working just five weeks?

Olympiad 41

1) When will the clock again show 2 o'clock?

2) The average of the five numbers is 6. What is their sum?

3) Compare the terms of the sequence with the multiples of 7 beginning with 7 itself.

4) What number multiplied by itself is 10,000?

5) Suppose each of the tables had just 2 people seated at it. How many seats will then be empty?

Olympiad 42

1) Suppose the cost of the seven books is exactly $8. Then what would be the exact cost of each book?

2) What is the sum of the digits of the first nine natural numbers? the next ten natural numbers?

3) What is the average amount that Alice earned for each of the five days?

4) How many small squares are in the figure? If the length of a side of a small square is s, what is the perimeter of the figure in terms of s?

5) How long would it take one person to complete half of the job?

Olympiad 43

1) Work backwards. If the registers ended up with the same amount, how much did each have before the transfer was made?

2) List all factors of 128. List the pairs of factors which have a product of 128. What other condition must be satisfied by one of the pairs?

3) Partition the figure into rectangles. There are many ways to do this. Two ways are shown below.

4) What value must H have?

5) How many more nickels than dimes were there to begin with?

Olympiad 44

1) List the multiples of 7 between 24 and 72. List the multiples of 6 between 24 and 72. What condition should you look for when you compare the two lists?

2) What values may B have? Replace B by one of these values and divide the three-digit number BBB by 6.

3) Work backwards to find how much Tom had when he entered the second store.

amount had	amount spent (1/3)	amount left(2/3)	
? ←	? ←	$12 ←	start here

4) Slice the tower into horizontal layers of cubes and find the number of cubes in each layer. You can also think of the tower as being constructed of vertical columns of cubes with each being built on a single cube. Count the number of cubes in each column starting with the tallest column.

5) B must be even since the number is divisible by 8. Since the number is also divisible by 11, there must be a five-digit number whose product with 11 is A9543B. Try B = 2 and fill in the blank spaces at the right to find A.

```
    P Q R S T
          * 1 1
    ─────────────
              2
      - - - -
            2
    - - - -
    ─────────────
    A 9 5 4 3 2
```

Olympiad 45

1) Calculate the number of sticks in each of the following in the order given: OCTA, OCTIL, OCTILLA.

2) What number should be placed in the lower right hand corner of the square?

3) How many points of the total 72 points were contributed by six field goals? subtract these points from 72. What does the remainder represent in terms of field goals and fouls?

4) If a side of the given square has length s, represent the total perimeter of the four congruent rectangles in terms of s.

5) The first equation can be rewritten as:
$$1 + 4 + 9 + 16 + \ldots + 625 = 5525$$

Rewrite the second equation in similar manner. Compare the terms of the left numbers of the two rewritten equations.

Olympiad 46

1) What is the largest amount that can be made?

2) If the entire group of 30 people consisted solely of children, how much would the tickets then cost? What accounts for the difference between the actual cost and this one?

3) Count the number of cubes in each horizontal layer of cubes starting at the top

4) What is the sum of the five numbers whose average is 16?

5) Observe that the first partial product (fpp) is a two-digit number. What is the largest value that AB may have? Examine the second partial product (spp). What values could C have? What is the smallest value that AB could have?

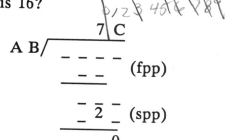

Olympiad 47

1) Calculate the cost of the 12 cans at the usual rate and again at the new rate.

2) List the numbers between 40 and 80 which satisfy condition c. According to condition b, what should the units digit be?

3) What is the average of the five consecutive numbers whose sum is 100?

4) How many steps should the dog take in covering the same distance that the cat covered in taking 12 steps?

5) What values may S have if N=6? Now determine the values for each of the following in the given order: H, E, I. Test each of your values for S.

Olympiad 48

1) List the triples so that the numbers in each triple are arranged according to size from smallest to largest. [(1,1,8) is the first triple to list.]

2) How much should we add to Rhoda's amount so that Rhoda and Patricia each have the same amount? Now do the same for Sara and Patricia.

3) What is the average height of all twelve columns?

4) Make a table:

Order:	1	2	3	4	5	6	7	8	9	10
Given Numbers:		8	?	?	14					?

What are the 3rd and 4th numbers of the sequence?

5) Make a list of the five largest possible share values less than $20. For each share value, find the corresponding number of members. Reread the conditions of the problem. The answer to the problem is contained in your list.

Olympiad 49

1) What is the largest three-digit number? Find the three-digit number that is closest to the largest three-digit number that is also divisible by 7 and by 8.

2) List the dimensions of some rectangles having perimeter 24 meters but different shapes. Find the area of each. Does the area change if the dimensions change?

3) Finding 1/3 of a number is the same as decreasing the number by what part of itself?

4) How much of the total charge of $3.45 represents the cost of shipping the number of pounds in excess of 5 pounds?

5) Multiply each of the second and third fractions of the sum by 10/10. Now change each of the three fractions to a decimal and add.

Olympiad 50

1) What is the first day of the year that has the same symbol in the U.S.A. and England? Find symbols for other days which each have the same symbol in the U.S.A. and in England.

2) Represent the two numbers as 6A and 6B. What is their product? Then what is the product of A and B?

3) How is the area of the walk related to the areas of the big and small rectangles seen in the diagram?

4) Make a diagram of the four numbers: 1/3 __ __ 1/2. How many increases are needed to go from 1/3 to 1/2?

5) Replace the circle in diagram 2 by its equal shown in diagram 1.

Solutions

1 Every 7 days from now will be Tuesday. Since 98 is a multiple of 7, the 98th day from now will be Tuesday. Then the 100th day from now will be **Thursday**.

2 **Method 1.** List the amounts in an organized manner.

				number of amounts
Amounts from 3¢-stamps:	3, 6, 9, 12			4
Amounts from 5¢-stamps:	5, 10, 15			3
Amounts from combining				
3¢-stamps and 5¢-stamps:	3+5,	3+10,	3+15	3
	6+5,	6+10,	6+15	3
	9+5,	9+10,	9+15	3
	12+5,	12+10,	12+15	3
			Total	19

Method 2.
The number of choices we have with respect to the 3¢-stamps is 5: we can use none, one, two, three, or four of the 3¢-stamps. This gives us a total of five choices. Similarly, we have four choices with respect to the 5¢-stamps: we can use none, one, two, or three of the 5¢-stamps. Each choice for the 3¢-stamps can be combined with one of the four choices we have for the 5¢-stamps. This gives a total of 20 combinations. However, this total includes the combination of no 3¢-stamps and no 5¢-stamps. Since the problem states that one or more of the stamps must be used, we exclude the combination of none of each. This then results in 20 – 1 or 19 combinations or amounts.

3 **Method 1.**

Arrange the numbers in a square array as shown. Add the numbers in the left column (or bottom row). The the sum of each of the other columns (or rows) can be easily determined by inspection. For example, each number in the second column is one more than its corresponding number in the first column. This is also true for other pairs of successive columns.

21	22	23	24	25	115
16	17	18	19	20	90
11	12	13	14	15	65
6	7	8	9	10	40
1	2	3	4	5	15
55	60	65	70	75	325

3 **Method 2.**
Notice that the sum of the numbers in the third column (or in the third row) is 65. This is the average of the sums of all five columns (or rows). Multiply this average by 5 to get the complete sum: 65 x 5 = 325.

Method 3.
Examine the array of numbers. Observe that the average of all numbers is the number in the middle of the array: 13. Then the sum must be 13 x 25 = 325.

Method 4.

$$S = 1 + 2 + 3 + \ldots + 23 + 24 + 25$$
$$\text{(reverse)} \quad S = 25 + 24 + 23 + \ldots + 3 + 2 + 1$$
$$\text{(add)} \quad 2S = 26 + 26 + 26 + \ldots + 26 + 26 + 26$$
$$2S = 26 \times 25$$
$$\text{Then} \quad S = 13 \times 25 \text{ or } 325$$

4 **Method 1.**
Combine both purchases: 5 pencils and 5 pens cost 150¢. Then 1 pencil and 1 pen cost 30¢, or 2 pencils and 2 pens cost 60¢. Since 3 pencils and 2 pens cost 72¢, then 1 pencil costs 12¢.

Method 2.
The difference in the prices of the two purchases is equivalent to the difference in the costs of a pen and a pencil. Therefore, a pen costs 6¢ more than a pencil, or, three pens cost 18¢ more than 3 pencils. Thus, the first purchase of 2 pencils and 3 pens is equivalent to the purchase of 2 pencils and 3 pencils plus 18¢, or 5 pencils plus 18¢. Since the cost of this purchase was 78¢, 5 pencils alone cost 60¢. Then 1 pencil had a cost of 12¢.

Method 3. Algebra
Let C = the cost of 1 pencil and N = the cost of 1 pen

Given . . . . (1)	$2C + 3N$	$= 78$
Given . . . . (2)	$3C + 2N$	$= 72$
Multiply both members of (2) by 3 . . . . (3)	$9C + 6N$	$= 216$
Multiply both members of (1) by 2 . . . . (4)	$4C + 6N$	$= 156$
Subtract (4) from (3) . . . . (5)	$5C$	$= 60$
Divide both members of (5) by 5 . . . . (6)	C	$= 12$

Answer: A pencil costs 12¢

5 Each person of the work crew of three people worked 20 days. Thus the number of individual work days needed to do the job was 60. Then each member of the work crew of four people must work 15 days in order to provide a total of 60 individual work days

Solutions

Olympiad 2

1 She paid out $10 + $20 = $30.
She received $15 + $25 = $40.
She made $10

2 **Method 1.**

Make a table. Let N = the number of nickels and Q the number of quarters. Start with 30 nickels and 0 quarters. Then in each successive line, decrease the number of nickels by 1 and increase the number of quarters by 1 thus keeping the total number of coins as 30. Notice that every time we decrease the number of nickels by 1 and increase the number of quarters by 1, we increase the preceding total value by 20¢.

N	Q	Total value in ¢
30	0	150
29	1	170 = 150 + 1 x 20
28	2	190 = 150 + 2 x 20
27	3	210 = 150 + 3 x 20
.	.	.
.	.	.
.	.	.
	?	410 = 150 + 260 = 150 + 13 x 20

Observe that the number of increases of 20 in the value column is the same as the number of quarters on the same line. To increase 150 in the value column to 410, we need to increase 150 by 260 or 13 x 20. Therefore there are 13 quarters and 17 nickels.

Method 2.
Let us look at the same problem in a different setting. Suppose 30 spiders had a total of 410 legs. Suppose further that some of the 30 spiders (nickelpeds) each have 5 legs and the others (quarterpeds) each have 5 rear legs and 20 forelegs. Suppose the nickelpeds always have their legs on the ground and the quarterpeds have just their 5 rear legs on the ground. Then the 30 spiders have just 150 legs on the ground and 260 legs in the air. But each quarterped has 20 legs in the air. Then there must be 260/20 = 13 quarterpeds. (Now compare method 1 and method 2; notice the similarities.)

2 **Method 3.** Algebra

Let N = the number of nickels and Q = the number of quarters.

Given . . . . (1)	N	+	Q	= 30
Given . . . . (2)	5N	+	25Q	= 410
Divide both members of (2) by 5 . . . . (3)	N	+	5Q	= 82
Subtract (1) from (3) . . . . (4)			4Q	= 52
Divide both members of (4) by 4 . . . . (5)			Q	= 13
Substitute from (5) into (1) . . . . (6)	N	+	13	= 30
Subtract 13 from both members of (6) . . . . (7)			N	= 17

Answer: There are 17 nickels and 13 quarters in the 30 coins.

3 **Method 1.**
Make a diagram of the sheet showing one 2" strip. Notice that there are twelve 2" by 3" pieces in the 2" strip. Since there are 12 strips of 2" in 24", there are 144 2" by 3" pieces in the 2' by 3' rectangle.

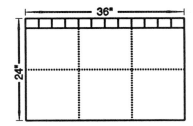

Method 2.
The area of one card is 6 square inches. The area of the sheet is 24 x 36 square inches. Divide 24 x 36 by 6; the answer is 144.

4 **Method 1.**
If the average of four scores is 145, then their sum is 4 x 145 = 580. The sum of the given scores is 139 + 143 + 144 = 426. Then the fourth score should be 580 – 426 = 154.

Method 2.
The first score is 6 less than the average; the second score is 2 less than the average; and the third score is 1 less than the average. Thus the sum of the three scores is 9 less than the sum of three average scores. Therefore, the fourth score needs to be 9 above the average score or 145 + 9 = 154.

4 **Method 3.** Algebra

Let S be the fourth score.

Then $\dfrac{139 + 143 + 144 + S}{4} = 145$, or

$$139 + 143 + 144 + S = 4(145)$$
$$426 + S = 580$$
$$S = 154$$

Answer: The fourth score is 154

5 Consider the frequency of appearance of the digit "1" in each of the places.

units place: the digit "1" appears once in every ten. Since 500 has 50 tens, the digit "1" will appear 50 times in the units place.

tens place: the digit "1" appears ten times in every hundred. Since 500 has 5 hundreds, the digit "1" will appear 50 times in the tens place.

hundreds place: the digit "1" will appear 100 times in the hundreds place (100, 101, 102, . . . , 199)

The digit "1" will appear a total of 200 times in the page numbers.

1 The least number of marbles that the set could have is the least common multiple of 2, 3, 4, 5, and 6.
$$LCM(2,3,4,5,6) = 60$$

2 The average speed for any trip is the total distance divided by the total time spent in traveling. The total distance was 120 miles and the total time was 5 hours.

Therefore the average speed = (120 miles)/(5 hours) = 24 miles/hour

Comment: It is interesting to observe that the average speed in this problem does not depend on the distance traveled. In other words, the average speed in this problem would be the same no matter what distance was traveled.

3 If a number is divisible by 9, then the sum of its digits is also divisible by 9. The digit sum is 3 + A + A + 1 = 4 + 2A. The digit sum cannot be 9 otherwise A = 2½. Therefore 4 + 2A = 18, and A = 7.

Olympiad 3

4 Any unit fraction whose denominator is the product of two consecutive numbers can be expressed as a difference of unit fractions in the following way:

$$\frac{1}{n(n+1)} = \frac{1}{n} - \frac{1}{n+1}$$

Example: $\quad \frac{1}{99 \times 100} = \frac{1}{99} - \frac{1}{100}$

Each of the fractions in the given sum can be expressed as the difference of two unit fractions like so:

$$\left[\frac{1}{1} - \frac{1}{2}\right] + \left[\frac{1}{2} - \frac{1}{3}\right] + \left[\frac{1}{3} - \frac{1}{4}\right] + \left[\frac{1}{4} - \frac{1}{5}\right] + \left[\frac{1}{5} - \frac{1}{6}\right]$$

Observe that when the addition is performed, all terms but the first and last drop out. Therefore the sum is:

$$1 - \frac{1}{6} \quad \text{or} \quad \frac{5}{6}$$

5 Since the successive terms of the sequence increase by 3, we consider the sequence to be related to multiples of 3 and display the following table:

order of terms	1	2	3	4	. . .	100
terms of sequence	1	4	7	10	. . .	?
multiples of 3	3	6	9	12		300

Compare each of the terms of the sequence with the multiple of 3 directly below it. Notice that each term of the sequence is 2 less than the corresponding multiple of 3 directly below it. Since the 100th multiple of 3 is 300, the corresponding term of the sequence is 300 − 2 = 298.

Olympiad 4

1 We need to know the number of boxes that were packaged in order to find the total selling price. The number of boxes is obtained by dividing 100 by 1¼. This is equal to 80. The total selling price is 80 x $1.75 which is equal to $140.

Olympiad 4

[2] The first partial product 114 is obtained from the product of AB and A; the second partial product is 304 and is obtained from the product of AB and B. It is clear that A is less than B.

Method 1.
Since the product of AB and A is 114, A is a divisor of 114. Therefore A may be 2, 3, or 6. Since AB x A = 114, A cannot be 2 because AB x A would be less than 60. Similarly A cannot be 6 since AB x A would be greater than 360. Therefore A must be 3. Then AB = 114/3 = 38. A = 3; B = 8.

Method 2.
From the first partial product 114, we see that B x A must end in 4. This can happen if A = 2 and B = 7, or A = 3 and B = 8, or A = 4 and B = 6. But 27 x 72 ≠ 3154, 46 x 64 ≠ 3154. However, 38 x 83 = 3154. Therefore A = 3 and B = 8.

Method 3.
From the second partial product 304, we see that B x B must end in 4. This can happen if B = 2 or B = 8. If B = 2, A = 1 since A is less than B. Then AB x BA = 12 x 21 which does not equal 3154. If B = 8 and AB x B = 304, then AB = 304/8 = 38. Therefore A = 3 and B = 8.

Method 4.
The two-digit number represented by AB is a factor of 114 and also of 304. Factor 114 and 304 completely: 114 = 2x3x19, 304 = 2x2x2x2x19 Since 2 and 19 are common factors of 114 and 304, then AB is either 19 or 2x19 = 38. Since 19x91 ≠ 3154 and 38x83 = 3154, A = 3 and B = 8.

[3] **Method 1.**

Make a diagram and draw 4 lines so that they intersect each other as shown. Count the sections. There are 11.

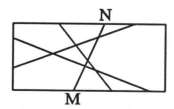

3 **Method 2.**
Make a table showing how many sections result when lines are added.

No. of lines	No. of Sections
1	2
2	4
3	7

Notice that the 2nd line added 2 sections to the previous total and that the 3rd line added 3 sections to the previous total. This suggests that the 4th line will add 4 sections to the previous total of 7, thus resulting in 11 sections.

Comment: To have the largest number of sections, each added line must intersect each of the existing lines at different points. If the lines do not intersect each other, it can be shown that there will be less sections. As indicated above, the nth line adds n sections to the previous total. As an example, let us add a fifth line to the diagram above and trace its path in our minds. The line starts from a point on the rectangle. When the line reaches the first line of the four existing lines, it has created a new section. When the line crosses the four existing lines, it creates 3 new sections. When the line continues from the 4th line of the existing lines to intersect the rectangle, another new section is created. Thus, the 5th line has added 1 + 3 + 1 new sections or a total of 5 new sections to the previous total of 11 sections.

4 Try A = 4.

Then $\frac{1}{3} = \frac{1}{4} + \frac{1}{B}$. This leads to: $\frac{1}{B} = \frac{1}{3} - \frac{1}{4}$ or $\frac{1}{12}$.

The following rule applies to all unit fractions:

$$\frac{1}{N} = \frac{1}{N+1} + \frac{1}{N(N+1)}$$

5 According to the order of operations, first perform the operation indicated in the parentheses.

$$6 * 8 = \frac{6 + 8}{2} \text{ or } 7.$$

Then $3 * (6 * 8) = 3 * 7 = \frac{3 + 7}{2}$ or 5.

Olympiad 5

1 **Method 1.**

The middle number of an odd number of consecutive numbers is always the average of the set. Then the average of the numbers is 320/5 or 64 which also is the third number or middle number. Count back by 2s.

Answer: The required number is 60.

Method 2.

Represent the middle number by n. Then the consecutive numbers can be represented by n− 4, n− 2, n, n+2, and n+4. The sum of the five numbers is 5n. Since 5n = 320, n = 64 and n− 4, the first number, is 60.

2 **Method 1.**

1 sq yd = 9 sq ft. Then 600 sq yd = 600x9 sq ft. Since 600 sq ft is 1/9 of 600x9 sq ft, the time required to mow 600 sq ft will be 1/9 of the time required to mow 600 sq yd. Thus 1/9 of 1½ hrs is 1/6 hr or 10 min.

Method 2.

Since 9 sq ft = 1 sq yd, 1 sq ft = 1/9 sq yd. Then the time needed to mow 1 sq ft is 1/9 of the time needed to mow 1 sq yd. Therefore, 600 sq ft will require 1/9 of 1½ hr or 1/6 hr or 10 min.

3 Work backward.

$$\cfrac{1}{2 + \cfrac{1}{2 + \cfrac{1}{2 + \cfrac{1}{2}}}} = \cfrac{1}{2 + \cfrac{1}{2 + \cfrac{1}{\frac{5}{2}}}} = \cfrac{1}{2 + \cfrac{1}{2 + \frac{2}{5}}} = \cfrac{1}{2 + \cfrac{1}{\frac{12}{5}}} = \cfrac{1}{2 + \frac{5}{12}} = \cfrac{1}{\frac{29}{12}} = \frac{12}{29}$$

4 If 4 is subtracted from 109, the result is 105. Then each of the two-digit numbers that will divide 109 with a remainder of 4 will divide 105 with no remainder. Thus, the problem is equivalent to finding all two-digit divisors of 105. Since the prime factors of 105 are 3, 5, and 7, the divisors are 3x5, 3x7, and 5x7, or 15, 21, and 35.

5 **Method 1.**

After some marbles are packaged in boxes for 12, the remaining marbles must be completely packaged in boxes for 5 with none left over. The following table shows what happens when some marbles are packaged in boxes for 12.

No. of boxes for 12	No. of marbles left over	No. of boxes for 5	Total no. of boxes
1	99-12 = 87	17; 2 m left over	--
*2	99-24 = 75	15	17
3	99-36 = 63	12; 3 m left over	--
⋮	⋮	⋮	⋮
*7	99-84 = 15	3	10

*Only in two cases (marked with an asterisk) can all 99 marbles be completely packaged in 12-marble and 5-marble boxes. However, only the first of these two cases will satisfy the condition that more than 10 boxes must be used. Thus 2 of the 12-marble boxes and 15 of the 5-marble boxes were used.

Method 2.

Let S denote the number of 5-marble boxes and L the number of 12-marble boxes. Then

$$5S + 12L = 99 \quad \text{or} \quad S = \frac{99 - 12L}{5}$$

In the second equation, 99 – 12L must be divisible by 5 if S is to be a whole number. This will happen only if L = 2 or 7. The corresponding values of S are 15 and 3. The number of boxes will be greater than 10 only when L = 2 and S = 15.

Olympiad 6

1 The largest value will occur when the denominator is as small as possible and the numerator is as large as possible. These conditions are satisfied when X is 50 and Y is 49. The largest value is $\frac{50 + 49}{50 - 49} = 99$.

2 **Method 1.**
T, the total number of chimes, equals $1 + 2 + 3 + 4 + \ldots + 10 + 11 + 12$. The sum of this series is 78.

Method 2.

$$1 + 2 + 3 + 4 + \ldots + 10 + 11 + 12$$
Reverse the series $\quad 12 + 11 + 10 + 9 + \ldots + 3 + 2 + 1$
Add both series $\quad 13 + 13 + 13 + 13 + \ldots + 13 + 13 + 13$

Each time we add a term and the corresponding term above, the sum is 13. There are 12 addends of 13 in the sum which is 156. But this is twice the sum of the first series. Therefore the total number of chimes in the twelve-hour period is 78.

Method 3.
The sum of the first six terms is 21:

$$1 + 2 + 3 + 4 + 5 + 6 = 21$$

The sum of the remaining terms can be represented as:

$$7 + 8 + 9 + 10 + 11 + 12 = (6+1)+(6+2)+(6+3)+(6+4)+(6+5)+(6+6)$$
$$= 6 \times 6 + (1 + 2 + 3 + 4 + 5 + 6)$$
$$= 36 + 21$$

The sum of the entire series therefore is $21 + 36 + 21 = 78$.

3 If the average of the five weights is 13 grams, then the total weight of the five weights is 5×13 or 65 grams. The sixth weight increases the total to 72 grams. The average of the six weights is 72/6 or 12 grams.

4 Since pennies are to be used in the selection, the number of pennies used must be a multiple of 5.

Case 1.

Suppose 5 pennies are selected. Then the remaining 16 coins must have a value of 95¢. The table at the right shows a pattern of values for the 16 coins. In the table, N stands for the number of nickels and D stands for the number of dimes. The last set of entries in the table satisfies the requirement that the 16 coins have a value of 95¢. Therefore 5 pennies, 13 nickels and 3 dimes satisfy the conditions.

N	D	Value
16	0	80¢
15	1	85¢
14	2	90¢
*13	3	95¢

Case 1 can also be solved by using algebra:

$$N + D = 16$$
$$5N + 10D = 95$$

See *Solutions*, Olympiad 2, Method 3, p. 102.

For another method of solving this pair of equations, see Method 2 in the above reference, p. 101.

Case 2. Suppose 10 pennies are selected. Then the remaining 11 coins must have a value of 90¢. Proceed as in Case 1. The reader will discover that 10 pennies, 4 nickels, and 7 dimes will satisfy the conditions.

Case 3. Suppose 15 pennies are selected. Then the remaining 6 coins must have a value of 85¢. But this is impossible since the largest value the remaining 6 coins could have is 60¢.

5

A Venn diagram is helpful in explaining the solution. Let an oval patch represent the set of students taking French and another oval represent those taking Spanish. In the diagram, observe that the intersection (overlap) of the two oval patches represents the set of students taking both French and Spanish (see region B). Region A represents the set taking French alone; region C represents the set taking Spanish alone; and D represents the set taking neither French nor Spanish. In the second Venn diagram, each x represents a student. Observe that the total number of x's in regions A, B, and C is 17. Therefore D has 13 students.

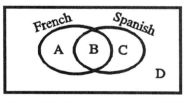

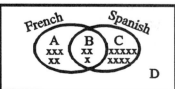

Olympiad 7

1

3 5 4	8 0 7	1 5 1 5
+ 4 5 3	+ 7 0 8	+ 5 1 5 1
X = 8 0 7	Y = 1 5 1 5	Z = 6 6 6 6

2 The following pairs of numbers represent the values of the two coins the boy could take from his pocket:

$$
\begin{array}{llll}
(1,1) & (1,5) & (1,10) & (1,25) \\
(5,5) & (5,10) & (5,25) & \\
(10,10) & (10,25) & &
\end{array}
$$

There are nine different pairs. Each pair has a sum that is different from the sum of each of the other pairs. The answer is 9.

3 Observe that each of the entries in the first column has the same remainder when it is divided by 7. The same can be said for each of the other columns. When 1,000 is divided by 7, the remainder is 6. Therefore 1,000 will appear in the column headed by F.

4 Since each person of the original group had 10 daily shares, the total supplies are equivalent to 120 daily shares. When 3 people join the group, the total number of people becomes 15. Then each person in the new group will have 120/15 or 8 daily shares. The supplies will last 8 days.

5 The area of each square is 176/11 or 16 square inches. The length of each side of a square is 4 inches. The perimeter of the U-shaped figure is equivalent to the total length of 24 sides or 96 inches.

Olympiad 8

1 Suppose I select 20 beads blindfolded. Among the 20 beads, there may be 5 beads of the same color. But it is also possible that the 20 beads may contain 4 beads of each color. Therefore I cannot be sure that there are 5 beads of the same color among the 20. However, the 21st bead guarantees that there are now at least 5 beads of the same color.

2 **Method 1.**

Think of the double of the number as six-thirds (6/3) of the number. Since the double of the number results when 20 is added to 1/3 of the number, 20 must be 5/3 the number. Then 1/5 of 20 must be equal to 1/5 of 5/3 of the number; or 4 is 1/3 of the number. Then 3 x 4 equals 3 x 1/3 of the number.

Answer: The required number is 12.

Method 2.

Let the double of the number be represented by the rectangle at the right. Divide the rectangle into 6 congruent sections, each one representing 1/3 of the number. Then 20 which is 5/3 of the number is represented by 5 boxes. Each of the boxes must have a value of 4. Since 3 boxes represent the number, the number must be 12.

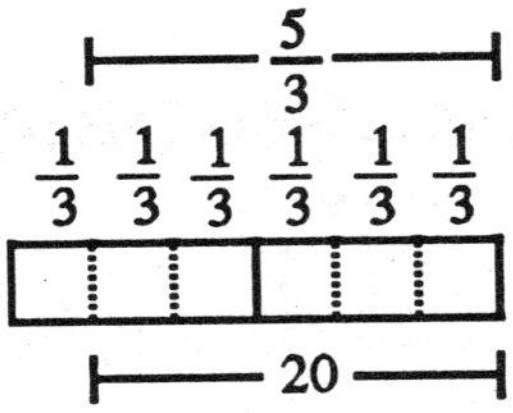

Method 3.

Let N denote the number. Then $\frac{N}{3} + 20 = 2N$ represents the condition of the problem. When solved, the equation yields the answer N = 12.

3 The are three different sizes for the squares that can be traced in the figure: 1x1, 2x2, and 3x3. The following table shows how many squares can be traced for each size.

Size of Square	Number of Squares
1x1	21
2x2	12
3x3	5
	total 38

4 **Method 1.**

Since $4 is 1/3 of what she had left after spending money, then $12 is 3/3 of what she had left after spending money. More simply, $12 is what she had left after spending money. But $12 is 1/3 of what she had to begin with. Then $36 is 3/3 of what she had to begin with; or, more simply, $36 is what she had to begin with.

Olympiad 8

4 **Method 2.**

Make a diagram showing the transactions. The rectangle represents all the money that was available at the outset.

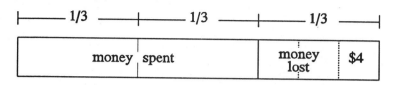

The amount of money that was left, $4, was 1/9 of the original amount of money. Then the original amount of money was $36.

Method 3.

Let M represent the amount of money the woman had at the start. Record the transactions as follows:

Amount	Spent	Money Left	Money Lost	Money Left
M	$\frac{2}{3}$M	$\frac{1}{3}$M	$\frac{2}{3}$ of $\frac{1}{3}$M or $\frac{2}{9}$M	$\frac{1}{3}$M $-$ $\frac{2}{9}$M or $\frac{1}{9}$M

Since $\frac{1}{9}$M = $4, M = $36. (The fractions in the above transactions can be avoided by letting the original amount be 9M.)

5 If a number is multiplied by 10, the product will have an additional terminal zero when written in standard form. If $1 \times 2 \times 3 \times \ldots \times 20$ is written as a product of prime factors, it will contain four 5's and more than four 2's among many factors. Then part of the product can be written as: $(5 \times 2)(5 \times 2)(5 \times 2)(5 \times 2)$ which can also be represented as $10 \times 10 \times 10 \times 10$. Therefore there are four terminal zeros in the product.

Olympiad 9

1 From the first column, we see that the sum for each row, column, and diagonal should be 90. Then the missing number in the 3rd row is 40, and the missing number in the lead diagonal is 30. The sum for the second column is $40 + 30 + x$ or $70 + x$. Then x must be 20.

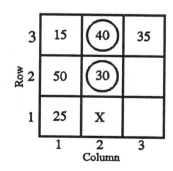

Olympiad 9

2 Arrange the terms of the given sequence in order. Since the terms of the sequence increase by 3s, also display the corresponding multiples of 3.

Order	1	2	3	4	. . .	?
Terms of Sequence	2	5	8	11	. . .	449
Multiples of 3	3	6	9	12	. . .	

Notice that each multiple of 3 is 1 more than the corresponding number of the sequence. Then the multiple of 3 that corresponds to 449 is 1 more than 449 or 450. Since 450 is the 150th multiple of 3, N must be 150.

3 If the perimeter is 22 inches, then the sum of the length and width, the semi-perimeter, is 11 inches. The table at the right shows what dimensions are possible and the resulting areas. Just 5 areas are possible.

One Side	Other Side	Area
10	1	10
9	2	18
8	3	24
7	4	28
6	5	30

4 It takes 2/3 of an hour or 40 minutes to drive from home to the shopping center. The return trip requires 5 minutes per mile. This gives a total of 100 minutes for the return trip. The total trip requires 140 minutes or 2 hours 20 minutes.

5 The product of 5 _ and B yields the second partial product 432. Then B is a divisor of 432. When we test 6, 8, and 9 as candidates for B by dividing each into 432, we get 432/6 = 72, 432/8 = 54, and 432/9 = 48. Of these results, only 54 can represent the divisor 5 _ . Observe that 54 x A is equal to the first partial product which is _ 6 _ in this case. The only value of A that satisfies this condition is 3. Therefore, A = 3 and B = 8.

Olympiad 10

1 In the tens column, H must be less than 3. Otherwise the sum would be a three-digit number. Therefore H = 1 or 2. In the units column, the sum of 4 Es is an even number. Then H in the sum must be 2. It follows that E must be either 3 or 8. If E = 8, the sum will be a three-digit number. Therefore E = 3, H = 2, and A = 9.

Olympiad 10

2 Examine the pairs of whole numbers whose product is 144.

144	72	48	36	24	18	16	12
1	2	3	4	6	8	9	12

The pair that has a difference of 10 is 18 and 8. Their sum is 26.

3 **Method 1.**
Observe that $\frac{A}{11}$ and $\frac{B}{3}$ must be proper fractions since their sum is a proper fraction. Therefore B must be less than 3; that is, either 1 or 2. Rewrite each fraction as an equivalent fraction with denominator 33.

$$(1) \quad \frac{3A}{33} + \frac{11B}{33} = \frac{31}{33}$$

If B = 1, 3A = 20. But A must be a whole number. Therefore B ≠ 1.
If B = 2, 3A = 9 and A = 3. Thus A = 3 and B = 2.

Method 2.
Rewrite equation (1) above as $\frac{3A + 11B}{33} = \frac{31}{33}$.

Then 3A + 11B = 31 and $A = \frac{31 - 11B}{3}$. B at most can be 2. Test B = 1 and

B = 2. Only the latter works. Then B = 2 and A = 3.

4 Since 121 = 11 x 11, the club has 11 members and each contributed 11¢. Each 11¢ share was paid in 3 coins which had to be 2 nickels and 1 penny. Then the 11 members each contributed 2 nickels or a total of 22 nickels.

5 **Method 1.**
For every 8 tests the student took, his average performance was: pass 7 and fail 1. On this basis he received 7x25¢ and paid 1x50¢ or $1.75-$.50 = $1.25 for each 8 tests. Since $1.25 is one-third of $3.75, he must have taken 3x8 or 24 tests, passed 21 and failed 3.

Method 2.
Let P = the number of tests passed and F = the number of tests failed.

Given . . . . (1)	P = 7F
Given . . . . (2)	25P − 50 F = 375
Divide both members of 2 by 25 . . . . (3)	P − 2F = 15
Substitute from (1) into (3) . . . . (4)	7F − 2F = 15
	or 5F = 15
Divide both members of (4) by 5 . . . . (5)	F = 3

Answer: The student failed 3 tests.

1 Statement in Problem   Order of Numerals

Statement in Problem	Order of Numerals
I before III but after IV	IV I III
II after IV but before I	IV II I III
V after II but before III	IV II V I III, or IV II I V III
V is not the third numeral	IV II I V III

2 Multiplicand

Since the units digit of the first partial product (fpp) is 2, the units digit of the multiplicand must be 6. The tens digit of the fpp is 8. This comes from multiplying the tens digit of the multiplicand by 7 and then adding to the product the "carry" of 4 (from 7x6). The tens digit of the multiplicand must be 2.

```
    4  2  6   multiplicand
       3  7   multiplier
  _____
    _  _  8  2   fpp
 1  2  _  _      spp
  _____
```

Multiplier

The tens digit of the multiplier must be 3 to give the second partial product (spp). Complete the multiplication. The product is 15,762.

3 **Method 1.**

Since Glenn likes neither baseball nor soccer, then tennis must be his favorite sport. Since Harry does not like baseball and cant like tennis (Glenn's favorite sport), then soccer is Harry's favorite. Glenn likes tennis, Harry likes soccer, and Kim must like baseball.

Method 2.

In the table at the right, G, H, and K represent Glenn, Harry, and Kim respectively; t, b and s represent tennis, baseball, and soccer. Enter N (for NO) in the table if the sport is not the associated person's favorite, and Y (for Yes) if it is. According to the given conditions, only one Y can appear in any row or column. Other letters in the row or column must be N.

	t	b	s
G	Y	N	N
H	N	N	Y
K	N	Y	N

4 Let a, b, c, d, and e represent the rays; and let (a,b) represent the angle formed by the rays a and b. Notice that (a,b) and (b,a) represent the same angle. The different angles that can be formed are: (a,b), (a,c), (a,d), (a,e), (b,c), (b,d), (b,e), (c,d), (c,e), (d,e). Therefore 10 different angles can be formed.

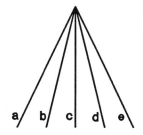

Method 2.
The angles could be listed according to size:
(a,b), (b,c), (c,d), (d,e)
(a,c), (b,d), (c,e)
(a,d), (b,e)
(a,e)

Method 3.
Make a diagram to show all possible pairings.

Each pairing is associated with the line segment joining two letters. Notice that there are 5x4 = 20 pairings. However, each pairing is repeated. For example, the pairing in the first of the five diagrams that represents (a,d) also appears in the fourth diagram as (d,a). Therefore we need to divide the total number of pairings in the above diagrams by 2. Thus, there are 10 different angles.

Comment: the methods described above are also applicable to a wide variety of problems involving tennis matches, chess matches, handshakes, etc.

5 **Method 1.**
Let P, A, and R represent the respective weights of a plum, apple and pear. The initial condition, 13P = 2A + 1R is shown as a balance of weights on a pan-balance. The solution will be obtained by removing the same weight from both sides of the pan-balance and by replacing a weight with its equivalent weight.

This is the initial condition:
(1) 13P = 2A + 1R

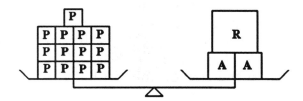

Olympiad 11

Since (2) 1R = 4P + 1A, replace R by 4P + 1A in the right side of the pan-balance. The diagram at the right shows what occurs:

(3) 13P = 3A + 4P

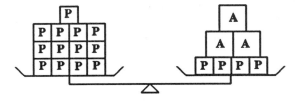

Remove 4P from both sides of the balance. The diagram at the right shows the result:

(4) 9P = 3A which is equivalent to 3P = A

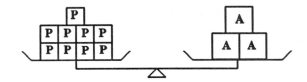

Substitute from (4) into (2). Then 1R = 4P + 3P or 7P.
A pear has the same weight as 7 plums.

Method 2.
The problem may also be solved by algebra without appealing to weights on a pan-balance.

Given . . . . (1)	13P	=	2A + 1R
Given . . . . (2)	1R	=	1A + 4P
Substitute for 1R (2) into (1) . . . . (3)	13P	=	2A + 1A + 4P
or	13P	=	3A + 4P
Subtract 4P from both members . . . . . (4)	9P	=	3A
Divide both members by 3 . . . . (5)	3P	=	1A
Substitute for 1A from (5) into (2) . . . (6)	1R	=	3P + 4P = 7P

Answer: 1 pear has the same weight as 7 plums.

Olympiad 12

1 Work backwards. Since the 3's are separated by 3 digits, then 3 must be either the first or the last digit of the six-digit number: 3 _ _ _ 3 _ or _ 3 _ _ _ 3. Since the 2's are separated by two digits, only the following placements can be made in the above arrangements of 3's: 3 _ 2 _ 3 2 or 2 3 _ 2 _ 3. The 1's occupy the remaining spaces: 3 1 2 1 3 2 or 2 3 1 2 1 3.

[2] Make a diagram:

From the diagram, yesterday was two days after Wednesday.
Answer: Yesterday was Friday.

[3] The following diagrams show the different paths that can be taken in going from A to C.

There are six different paths.

[4] **Method 1.**
Make a table in which the number of nickels (N) and the number of dimes (D) totals 16.

Suppose all 16 coins are nickels.

Exchange 1 nickel for 1 dime. The value increases 5¢.

Repeat the exchange until the desired total value of 100¢ is reached.

The desired value is reached on this line.

N	D	Total Value
16	0	80
15	1	85 = 80 + 1x5
14	2	90 = 80 + 2x5
13	3	95 = 80 + 3x5
12	4	100 = 80 + 4x5

Observe that the number of dimes is the same as the number of increases of 5 in the total value column on the same line. The answer can be obtained after completing the second line of the table by observing that the number of dimes needed to reach 100¢ is the same as the number of 5's by which 80 must be increased in order to reach 100.

4 **Method 2.**
Instead of nickels and dimes, think of nickelpeds (spiders which have 5 legs on the ground) and dimepeds (spiders which have 10 legs, 5 on the ground and 5 in the air at all times). Instead of 100¢, think of 100 legs. Now transform the problem into: There are 16 spiders consisting of nickelpeds and dimepeds with a total of 100 legs. How many spiders of each kind were there? Since each spider has 5 legs on the ground, there are 80 legs on the ground. Then there must be 20 legs in the air. Since each dimeped has 5 legs in the air, there must be 20/5 = 4 dimepeds. It follows that there are 12 nickelpeds.

Method 3.
Let N the number of nickels and D the number of dimes.

Given . . . . (1)	$N + D = 16$	
Given . . . . (2)	$5N + 10D = 100$	
Divide both sides of (2) by 5 . . . . (3)	$N + 2D = 20$	
Subtract members of (1) from (3) . . . . (4)	$D = 4$	
Substitute from (4) into (1) . . . . (5)	$N + 4 = 16$	
Subtract 4 from both members . . . . (6)	$N = 12$	

Answer: The number of nickels is 12, the number of dimes is 4.

5 Let N be the required number. Notice that when N is divided by 4, 5, or 6, the remainder is 3 less than the divisor in each case. If N is increased by 3, this new number will be divisible by 4, 5, and 6 without remainder. The smallest number that the new number, N+3, can be is the least common multiple of 3, 4, and 5 which is 60. Since 60 is 3 more than the required number, the number is 57.

1 Make a table of the number of different squares that can be obtained for each of the following types of squares: 1 by 1, 2 by 2, 3 by 3.

Size of Squares	Number
1 by 1	15
2 by 2	6
3 by 3	1
	Total 22

2 The product of the first multiplication, C x C, has a units digit which is also C. Then C may have the values 1, 5, or 6.

Case 1. Suppose C = 1. Then the product must be ABC. However the product is DBC. Reject the assumption that C = 1.

Case 2. Suppose C = 5. Then A = 1. Otherwise, the product would be a four-digit number. Notice that when the tens digit B of the multiplicand is multiplied by 5 and the "carry" of 2 is added, the result should have a units digit of B. This will occur when B = 2 or 7. If B = 2, then D = 6. If B = 7, then D = 8. Thus, there are two answers: A=1, B=2, C=5, D=6, or A=1, B=7, C=5, D=8.

Case 3. Suppose C = 6. Then A = 1. Otherwise the product will have four digits. When B of the multiplicand is multiplied by 6 and the "carry" of 3 is added, the result should have a units digit of B. It can be shown that this is impossible. Reject the assumption that C = 6.

[3] The average of the first and third numbers is the second number. The average of the first and third numbers is their sum divided by 2: average = 118/2 = 59. The three numbers are: 58, 59, 60.

Comment: For any 3 consecutive numbers, the average of the first and third number is the second number. We show this in the following way. Let the three numbers be N−1, N, and N+1. The average of the first and third numbers is :

$$\frac{(N-1) + (N+1)}{2} = \frac{2N}{2} = N.$$

In a similar way we can show that the average of the three numbers is also N:

$$\frac{(N-1) + N + (N+1)}{3} = \frac{3N}{3} = N.$$

[4] In the discussion that follows, let A = the amount that Anne has, B = the amount that Betty has, and C = the amount that Cynthia has.

Method 1.
The three conditions of the problem can be represented by (1) A + B = 12, (2) B + C = 18 and (3) A + C = 10.
   From (1) and (2) it is clear that C = A + 6.
   From (2) and (3), it is clear that B = A + 8.
   It follows that A is the smallest amount.

Make a table of values for A, B, and C. Check out conditions (1), (2) and (3) against the values in the table.

When A = 1, conditions (1), (2) and (3) are not true.

When A = 2, conditions (1), (2) and (3) are true.

A	B (A + 8)	C (A + 6)
1	9	7
2	10	8

Answer: Anne had the least amount which was $2.

4 **Method 2.**

If we add the given amounts, we get $12 + $18 + $10 = $40. This is double the sum of what each girl had. Then the sum of what each had was $20. From condition (2), B + C = 18, A must be 2.

Method 3. Algebra

Given . . . . (1)	A + B = 12
Given . . . . (2)	B + C = 18
Given . . . . (3)	A + C = 10
Add the members of (1), (2), and (3) . . . . (4)	2A + 2B + 2C = 40
Divide both members of (4) by 2 . . . . (5)	A + B + C = 20
Subtract members of (2) from those of (5) (6)	A = 2

Answer: Anne had the least amount which was $2.

5 **Method 1.**

The different ways 15 pennies can be distributed into 4 piles are (1,2,3,9), (1,2,4,8), (1,2,5,7), (1,3,4,7), (1,3,5,6), (2,3,4,6). Thus, the number of pennies in the largest pile of each distribution may be 6, 7, 8, or 9. The smallest of these is 6.

Method 2.

To find the smallest possible number of pennies in the largest pile, make the sum of the numbers of pennies in the other three piles as large as possible. This occurs when the first three piles contain 1, 3, and 5 pennies, or 2, 3, and 4 pennies.

Olympiad 14

1 The sum of the length and width is the semi-perimeter, 10 feet. The following table gives the possible lengths and widths.

Length	9	8	7	6	5
Width	1	2	3	4	5

There are five rectangles which have different shapes, perimeter of 20 feet, and sides whose foot-measure is a whole number.

2 **Method 1.**

The maximum score of 50 occurs when all ten answers are correct. For each incorrect answer, one has to deduct 7 points from the maximum score; 5 points for the loss of the problem score and 2 points for the incorrect answer. Since Nancy scored 29 points, 21 points were deducted for incorrect answers. This represents 3 incorrect answers. Then Nancy had 7 correct answers.

Method 2.

Make a table. Let C represent the number correct and I represent the number incorrect.

C	I	Total Points
10	0	50
9	1	43 = 50 – 1x7
8	2	36 = 50 – 2x7
7	3	29 = 50 – 3x7

When Nancy has 7 correct answers (and 3 incorrect answers), her total score is 29 points.

Notice that the number of incorrect problems in the table is the same as the number of 7's subtracted from 50 on the same line under the total points column.

Method 3. Algebra

Given . . . . (1)	$C + I = 10$	
Given . . . . (2)	$5C - 2I = 29$	
Multiply both members of (1) by 2 . . . . (3)	$2C + 2I = 20$	
Add the members of (2) and (3) . . . . (4)	$7C = 49$	
Divide both members of (4) by 7 . . . . (5)	$C = 7$	

3 **Method 1.**

Notice that the order of entries in the table is reversed on the even rows. Take the 3rd and 4th entries in the C column and divide each by 8. The remainders are 3 and 6 respectively. These remainders also happen to be the first two entries in column C. The same relationship occurs in each of the columns if we consider 8 in column A to be equivalent to a remainder of 0. When 101 is divided by 8, the remainder is 5. Therefore 101 will appear in column D.

A	B	C	D
1	2	3	4
8	7	6	5
9	10	11	12
....		14	13

Method 2.

Each group of 8 consecutive numbers, beginning with 1, is arranged the same way in the table. If 101 is divided by 8, we get 12 and a remainder of 5. Interpret this as 12 groups of 8 and 1 partial group of 5. The partial group will have 97 as its first number in column A. Show the partial group in the table as shown at the right. The number appears in column D.

A	B	C	D
97	98	98	100
....			101

Method 3.

Arrange each group of 8 consecutive numbers on one line by repeating the column headings in reverse order as shown at the right. The 12th group will begin with 97, and 101 will be in the D column.

A	B	C	D	D	C	B	A
1	2	3	4	5	6	7	8
9	10	11	12	13	14	15	16

97	98	99	100	101			

4 In one hour, the first pipe will fill 1/8 of the pool, the second pipe 1/12, and the third pipe 1/24. Together, in one hour, they will fill 1/8 + 1/12 + 1/24 of the pool. This is equivalent to 1/4 of the pool in one hour. Therefore the three pipes will fill the pool in 4 hours.

Olympiad 14

5 Observe that the entries in the right diagonal have a sum of 34. Then the entry in column 3, row 1 should be 2, the entry in column 4, row 1 should be 13, and the entry in column 4, row 3 should be 6. The sum of the entries in row 3 is $N+19$. N must be 15.

4			7	12
3	N	4	9	⑥
2		5	16	3
1	8	11	②	⑬

Row / Column 1 2 3 4

N can also be determined by finding the entry in column 1, row 2 which is 10, the entry in column 2, row 4 which is 14, and the entry in column 1, row 4 which is 1. The sum of the four entries in column 1 is $N+19$. N is therefore 15.

Olympiad 15

1 **Method 1.**
Sum the consecutive natural numbers begining with 1 until a total of 78 is reached.

$$1 + 2 + 3 + 4 + 5 + 6 + 7 + 8 + 9 + 10 + 11 + 12 = 78$$

Therefore, the train will be full after 12 stops. It would be helpful in this case if the reader knew the sum of the first 10 natural numbers which is 55. Since 55 + 11 + 12 = 78, the problem is readily solved.

Method 2.
To find the sum of an arithmetic series, multiply the average value of the terms of the series by the number of terms. The average value is easily obtained by dividing the sum of the first and last terms of the series by 2.[1]

series	average	×	no. of terms	=	sum
$1 + 2 + 3 + \ldots + 10$	$\frac{1 + 10}{2}$	×	10	=	55
$1 + 2 + 3 + \ldots + 10 + 11$	$\frac{1 + 11}{2}$	×	11	=	66
$1 + 2 + 3 + \ldots + 10 + 11 + 12$	$\frac{1 + 12}{2}$	×	12	=	78

---

[1] For a more detailed treatment of sums of series, see: Lenchner, G. <u>Creative Problem Solving in School Mathematics,</u> Houghton Mifflin Co., 1983, pp. 75-81, 289-290.

2 **Method 1.**
Those cubes marked by a circle have paint on one or more faces. The third layer is like the second layer; the fourth layer is like the first. The first layer has 16 cubes with paint on one or more faces; the second layer has 12 cubes with paint on one or more layer faces. Therefore there are 56 cubes with paint on one or more faces. Since the entire cube contains 64 1-inch cubes, there are 8 1-inch cubes which do not have paint on any face.

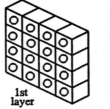
1st layer

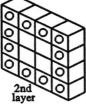
2nd layer

Method 2.
The outer cubes of the 4-inch cube have paint on one or more faces. If these cubes are removed, the remaining figure is a 2-inch cube. A 2-inch cube contains 8 1-inch cubes. These cubes do not have paint on any face.

3 **Method 1.**
A purchase of $10 can be paid for with 5 two-dollar bills or with 2 five-dollar bills. The $10 purchase paid for with two-dollar bills requires 3 more bills than the $10 purchase paid for with five-dollar bills. Since it is given that the number of two-dollar bills needed for a purchase is 9 more than the number of five-dollar bills needed for the purchase, the value of the purchase must be equivalent to 3 purchases of $10 or a total of $30.

Method 2.
Let T = number of two-dollar bills and F = number of five-dollar bills. We seek a purchase for which $T - F = 9$.

Amount of Purchase	T	F	T–F
$10	5	2	3
$20	10	4	6
* $30	15	6	9

Method 3.
Let N be the number of five-dollar bills needed for the purchase. Then N + 9 is the number of two-dollar bills needed for the same purchase. The value of the purchase is 5N or 2(N + 9).

Given . . . . (1)	$5N$	$= 2(N + 9)$
Expand the right member of (1) . . . . (2)	$5N$	$= 2N + 18$
Subtract 2N from both members of (2) . . . (3)	$3N$	$= 18$
Divide both members of (3) by 6 . . . . (4)	N	$= 6$

Since 6 five-dollar bills are needed, the value of the purchase is $30.

4 **Method 1.**
Let the tank be represented by the diagram at the right in which each box represents 1/4 of the tank's capacity. Observe that 3/4 of the tank contains 24 gallons. Then 1/4 of the tank contains 8 gallons. Therefore 4/4 or a full tank contains 32 gallons.

Method 2.
If 3/4 of the tank contains 24 gallons, then 1/4 of the tank contains 1/3 of 24 or 8 gallons. Then 4/4 or a full tank contains 4x8 or 32 gallons.

Method 3.
Let N represent the gallon-capacity of the tank.

Given: . . . . (1) $\quad \dfrac{3}{4} N = 24$

Multiply both members of (1) by $\dfrac{4}{3}$: . . . . . . (2) $\quad \dfrac{4}{3} \times \dfrac{3}{4} N = \dfrac{4}{3} \times 24$

Simplify both members: . . . . (3) $\quad N = 32$

The capacity of the tank is 32 gallons.

5

Make a table of the end-digits of completed multiplication strings. Notice that the end-digits repeat in groups of four. Since thirty-five 3's will appear on the 35th line of the table, and since thirty-five equals 8 groups of 4 plus 3, the end digit will be the same as end-digit of line 3 which happens to be 7.

String	End-Digit
3	3
3x3	9
3x3x3	7
3x3x3x3	1
3x3x3x3x3	3
3x3x3x3x3x3	9
3x3x3x3x3x3x3	7
.	.
.	.
.	.

Olympiad 16

1   Three weeks or 21 days before Friday the 25th is Friday the 4th. Count back to the first day.

Answer: The first day of the month is Tuesday.

2   **Method 1.**

Let AB represent the age of the man and BA represent the age of the wife. The given conditions can be expressed as:

$$\begin{array}{r} (1) \quad A\,B \\ +\,B\,A \\ \hline 9\,9 \end{array} \qquad \begin{array}{r} (2) \quad A\,B \\ -\,B\,A \\ \hline 9 \end{array}$$

From (1), the sum of A and B is 9. From (2), B is 1 less than A. In other words, A and B are consecutive numbers whose sum is 9. Then A = 5, B = 4. The man is 54 years old; his wife is 45.

Method 2.

The sum of the digits of the man's age must be 9. Since the man is older than his wife, A is greater than B. Test two-digit numbers whose digit-sum is 9. When the difference between the man's age and his wife's age is 9, the man's age is the required age.

Man's Age	81	72	63	54
Wife's Age	18	27	36	45
Difference	63	45	27	9

Method 3.

Let M = the man's age and W = the wife's age.

Given . . . . (1)	M + W	=	99
Given . . . . (2)	M − W	=	9
Add members of (1) and (2) . . . . (3)	2M	=	108
Divide both members of (3) by 2 . . . . (4)	M	=	54

The man's age is 54.

3   Going to the fair, 12 people rode in the buggies. Since 3 people rode in each buggy, there were 4 buggies. On the return trip, 4 people rode in each buggy. Then 16 people rode in the buggies. Since the total number of people was 21, 5 rode in the coach.

4 From the first and third views, the letters on the faces adjacent to H are A, Y, X, N. Then the remaining letter E is opposite H. Similarly, from the second and third views, the letters on the faces adjacent to X are E, Y, H, N. Then the remaining letter A is opposite X. The letters which have not been paired are Y and N. They must be opposite each other.

5 Let D = the sum of the odd numbers from 1 through 99. Let N = the sum of the even numbers from 2 through 98.

$$
\begin{array}{rcl}
D & = & 1 + 3 + 5 + 7 + \ldots + 97 + 99 \\
N & = & (0) + 2 + 4 + 6 + \ldots + 96 + 98 \\
\hline
D - N & = & 1 + 1 + 1 + 1 + \ldots + 1 + 1
\end{array}
$$

The difference D – N is the sum of fifty 1's.
(Notice that the sum of the even numbers is not changed by adding zero to the series. It does permit us to pair the numbers of both series 1 to 1.)

1 We have to find 7 coins whose value is 25¢. If the coins were nickels, their total value would be too great. There must be at least 5 pennies. Then we need two coins whose value is 20¢. The coins are dimes. Therefore the remaining coins are 5 pennies and 2 dimes.

2 **Method 1.**

If 2 loaves and 4 rolls cost $2.40, then 1 loaf and 2 rolls cost $1.20. Since 1 loaf and 6 rolls cost $1.80, then 4 rolls cost 60¢ or 15¢ each. Now the cost of a loaf can be determined from either transaction. One loaf and 6 rolls cost $1.80, but the 6 rolls cost 6x15 or 90¢. Therefore the loaf must cost 90¢.

Method 2.
Let L = the cost of a loaf in cents and R = the cost of a roll in cents.

Given . . . . (1)	$L + 6R = 180$
Given . . . . (2)	$2L + 4R = 240$
Divide the members of (2) by 2 . . . . (3)	$L + 2R = 120$
Subtract the members of (3) from (1) . . . . . (4)	$4R = 60$
Divide both members of (4) by 4 . . . . (5)	$R = 15$
Replace R by 15 in (3) . . . . (6)	$L + 30 = 120$
Subtract 30 from both members of (6) . . . . . (7)	$L = 90$

A loaf cost 90¢.

Solutions

3 Let S = the inch-length of one side of a small box. The perimeter of figure A is 16xS which equals 48. Then S = 3. The perimeter of figure B = 20xS, or 20x3 = 60.

4 **Method 1.**
Since the number of children is 3 more than a multiple of 4, that number could be 7, 11, 15, 19, 23, 27, 31, 35, 39, 43, . . . Since the nunber of children is 2 less than a multiple of 5, the number could be 3, 8, 13, 18, 23, 28, 33, 38, 43, . . . Some of the numbers that satisfy both conditions are 23, 43, 63, 83, and so forth. The smallest of these numbers is 23. Thus, there are 23 children in the class.

Method 2.
Let N = the number of benches in the classroom. Then the number of children can be expressed as 4N + 3 or 5N – 2.

Given . . . . (1)   4N + 3 = 5N – 2
Subtract 4N from both members of (1) . . (2)   3 = N – 2
Add 2 to both members of (2): . . . . (3)   5 = N
The number of benches in the classroom is 5.
The number of children is 4x5 + 3 or 23.

5 In the units column, notice that the sum of A, B, and C ends in B. Then A + C = 10. Since A is also the tens digit of the sum, A must be 1. Therefore C = 9.

1 **Method 1.**
The average of the two weights is 69. The heavier boy is 17 more than the average or 69 + 17 = 86, and the lighter boy is 17 less than the average or 69 – 17 = 52.

Method 2.
Let H = the weight of the heavier boy and L = the weight of the lighter boy. Then:

$$H + L = 138 \text{ and}$$
$$H - L = 34$$

By addition $2H = 172$ or $H = 86$.

Solutions

2 If page numbers are in the 40's, then the product is greater than 1,600. If the page numbers are in the 50's, then the product is greater than 2,500. Clearly the page numbers are in the 40's. Since the two page numbers are consecutive numbers, the units digits must be 2 and 3 or 7 and 8. Try 42 and 43. They work!

3 Just the shaded cubes have 4 red faces.
The other cubes have either 3 or 5 red faces.

4 Since 13 x 13 = 169, the club has 13 members and each contributed 13¢ in 5 coins. The 5 coins had to consist of 3 pennies and 2 nickels. Thus 26 nickels were contributed by the 13 members.

5 The average of the set of the consecutive numbers, 15, is also the middle number. Thus there are 7 consecutive numbers before 15 and 7 consecutive numbers after 15. The 7 numbers before 15 begin with 8: 8, 9, 10, 11, 12, 13, 14. The average of the first 5 numbers (8, 9, 10, 11,12) is the middle number, which is 10.

Olympiad 19

1 **Method 1.**
The average cost of the camera and case is $50. Since the camera and case differ in cost by $90, they each differ from the average cost by $45. Therefore the camera will cost $50 + $45 or $95, and the case costs $50 – $45 or $5. Notice that these results satisfy the given conditions: the total cost is $100 and the difference in costs is $90. See the diagram at the right.

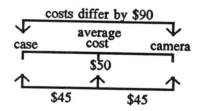

Method 2.
Let M = the cost of the camera and S = the cost of the case. The two conditions of the problem may then be expressed in the following way.

Given . . . . (1)	M + S	= 100
Given . . . . (2)	M – S	= 90
Add the members of (1) and (2) . . . . (3)	2M	= 190
Divide both members of (3) by (2) . . . . (4)	M	= 95
Replace M in (1) by 95 . . . . (5)	95 + S	= 100
Subtract 95 from both members of (5) . . . . (6)	S	= 5

The case cost $5.

2 From the second addition, B = 7. From the first addition C = 5. Then A = 4.
Answer: A = 4, B = 7, C = 5.

3 **Method 1.**[2]
From the first and second conditions (1) K+L = 11 and (2) L+M = 19, M is 8 more than K. From the second and third conditions (2) L+M = 19 and (3) K+M = 16, L is 3 more than K. Make a table of values for K, L, and M. Check out conditions (1), (2), and (3) against the values found in the table.

K	L (K+3)	M (K+8)	
1	4	9	Fails to satisfy the conditions
2	5	10	Fails to satisfy the conditions
3	6	11	Fails to satisfy the conditions
4	7	12	*Satisfies the given conditions*

12 points are assigned to M.

Method 2.
Instead of using the table in Method 1, we could use the conclusion that L is 3 more than K, L = K + 3 and replace L in condition (1), K + L = 11. Then condition (1) becomes:
$$K + (K + 3) = 11, \text{ or } 2K + 3 = 11.$$
By simple algebraic techniques, the solution is K = 4. Since M is 8 more than K, M = 12.

Method 3.
If we add the given amounts, we get 11 + 19 + 16 = 46. This sum contains the double of K, L and M. Then K + L + M = 23. Since K + L = 11, then M = 12.

Method 4. Algebra.

Given . . . . (1)	K	+ L			= 11
Given . . . . (2)		L	+	M	= 19
Given . . . . (3)	K		+	M	= 16
Add the members of (1), (2), (3) . . . . (4)	2K	+ 2L	+ 2M		= 46
Divide both members of (4) by 2 . . . . (5)	K	+ L	+ M		= 23
Subtract members of (1) from those of (5) . (6)			M		= 12

Answer: 12 points are assigned to M.

---

[2] For a similar problem in a different setting, see Olympiad 13, problem 4.

Olympiad 19

4 **Method 1.**

Work backwards. Mrs. Winthrop had $10 before her last purchase in the second store. This is half of what she had when she entered the store. Therefore she had $20 when she entered the second store. This is also what she had when she left the first store. Before she made her last purchase in the first store, she had $10 more than $20, or $30. But $30 is half of what she had when she entered the first store. She must have had $60 when she entered the first store.

Method 2.

Make a diagram of what happened in the two stores working backward.

	amount had when entering store	amount had before last purchase	amount left over	
second store	20	10	0	Start Here
first store	60	30	20	

5 If a number is divisible by 72, it is also divisible by 8 and by 9. Rewrite the number A4273B as the following sum:

$$A42000 + 73B$$

A42000 is divisible by 8 (any multiple of 1000 is divisible by 8). Then 73B has to be divisible by 8 if the entire number is divisible by 8. B has to be 6.

If a number is divisible by 9, the sum of its digits is also divisible by 9. Therefore, A + 4 + 2 + 7 + 3 + 6 or A + 22 is a multiple of 9. The smallest multiple of 9 which is greater than 22 is 27. Then A + 22 = 27, or A = 5.

Olympiad 20

1 **Method 1.**

The train moves 3 miles in 3x(1 min 20 sec) which is equal to 4 minutes. There are 15 groups of 4 minutes in 1 hour. Therefore the train moves 15 x 3 miles or 45 miles in 15 x 4 minutes or 1 hour.

Method 2.

For every 1⅓ minutes in 1 hour, the train moves 1 mile.

$$60 \text{ minutes} \div 1\tfrac{1}{3} \text{ minutes} = 60 \times \frac{3}{4} = 45.$$

Therefore, the train travels 45 miles in 1 hour.

2 Since the remainder is 1 when the number is divided by 3 or 5, the remainder is also 1 when the number is divided by 15. Then the number has to be one of the following: 16, 31, 46, 61, 76, or 91. The last of these is divisible by 7 without remainder.

3 Examine the following table of train lengths.

Total train-length	No. of 6-inch trains	No. of 7-inch trains
30 inches	5	0
31 inches	4	1
32 inches	3	2
33 Inches	2	3

Only the first train length, 29 inches, cannot be made by a hook-up.

4 In 10 minutes, A travels 7,000 yards, B travels 8,000 yards, and C travels 9,000 yards. At that time, each is at the starting point and together again for the first time since they started the race.

5 **Method 1.**
Make a table of some of the costs the ruler might have.

Cost of ruler	Alice's amount	Betty's amount	Sum of amounts
22¢	0¢	19¢	19¢
23¢	1¢	20¢	21¢
24¢	2¢	21¢	23¢
25¢	3¢	22¢	25¢

If the ruler costs 25¢, together they will have enough to purchase the ruler. The most the ruler could cost if they together do not have enough money to purchase the ruler is 24¢.

Method 2.
Suppose the ruler costs R cents. Then Alice has (R–22) cents, Betty has (R–3) cents, and together they have (2R–25) cents. But this sum is still not enough to pay for the ruler; that is,

$$2R-25 < R, \text{ or}$$
$$R < 25.$$

Since R is less than 25, the most it could be is 24.

Olympiad 21

1 **Method 1.**
One nickel and one dime have a total value of 15¢. If $6.00 is divided by $.15, the result is 40. Therefore there are 40 nickels (and 40 dimes) in $6.00.

Method 2. (Trial and Error)
A set of ten dimes and ten nickels is worth $1.50. Four such sets are worth $6.00. Therefore, there are 40 nickels in the $6.00.

Method 3.
Let N represent the number of nickels and also the number the number of dimes. The ¢-value of the nickels is 5N and the ¢-value of the dimes is 10N. Since the sum of these values is 600¢, we write:

$$5N + 10N = 600 \quad \text{or}$$
$$15N = 600$$
$$\text{Then} \quad N = 40$$

2 When A is multiplied by 7, the result is a number whose unit's digit is A. The only digits which satisfy this condition are 0 and 5. If A = 0, then B = 0 which contradicts the qiven conditions. Therefore A = 5. Since B times 7 with a "carry" of 3 also ends in 5, then B = 6.

The reconstructed problem is:
$$\begin{array}{r} 6\ 5 \\ 7 \\ \hline 4\ 5\ 5 \end{array}$$

Answer: A + B + H = 5 + 6 + 4 = 15.

3 The number of packages of cheese $= 350 \div 1\frac{3}{4}$ or $\dfrac{350}{1\frac{3}{4}}$

Selling price = the number of packages x $1.75

Selling price $= \dfrac{350}{1\frac{3}{4}} \times \$1.75 = \$350$. (Note that $1\frac{3}{4} = 1.75$)

4 Each of the 4 corner cubes has 4 red faces. Each of the 8 other cubes on the edges has 3 red faces. Each of the 4 central cubes has 2 red faces. Then, each of the corner cubes and each of the central cubes has an even number of red faces. There are 8 such cubes.

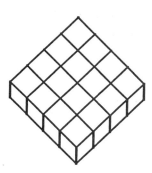

Olympiad 21

5 **Method 1.**
Suppose the share of the youngest is ⬚$. Then each of the other brothers, in order of age, gets:

⬚$ + \$100, ⬚$ + \$200, ⬚$ + 300.

Together the four brothers get:
⬚$ + ⬚$ + ⬚$ + ⬚$ + \$100 + \$200 + \$300, or more simply
$$4 ⬚\$ + \$600.$$
But 4 ⬚$ + \$600 = \$1200. Then 4 ⬚$ = \$600 and ⬚$ = \$150.
Answer: The share of the youngest is \$150.

Method 2.
If the money was divided equally among the brothers, they would each get \$300 which is the average. Since the oldest gets \$300 more than the youngest, he gets \$150 more than the average, and the youngest gets \$150 less than the average. Then the share of the youngest is \$300 – \$150 or \$150.

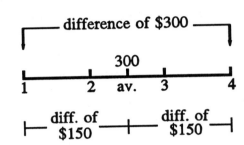

Note that in the above graphic representation of the shares, 1 is the smallest and 4 is the largest.

Olympiad 22

1 Today is Tuesday. 365 days from now is equivalent to 52 weeks and 1 day. 52 weeks from today is also Tuesday. The next day is Wednesday.

2 Work backward.

The result is (28 x 3 – 8) ÷ 4 = 19. The starting number should be 19.

3 **Method 1.**
The square region has an area of 4 square feet or 576 square inches. The tile has an area of 6 square inches. Then 576 ÷ 6 = 96. Answer: the least number of tiles needed to cover a square 2 feet on each side is 96.

3 **Method 2.**
Separate the square into twelve strips each 2 inches wide.

One Strip: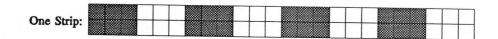

The number of 2 by 3 tiles in one strip is 8. Since there are twelve strips, there are 12 x 8 = 96 tiles in the twelve strips.

4 The total score has to be greater than or equal to 6 x 3 = 18, and less than or equal to 6 x 7 = 42. Therefore neither of the scores 16 and 44 can be obtained. Since the point-value assigned to each of the three regions is odd, the sum of any pair of the given point-values is even. Then the sum of any six scores (3 pairs of scores) is also even. It follows that the scores 19, 31, and 41 cannot be obtained. Only 26 is possible and can be obtained in any of the following ways: (3,3,3,3,7,7), (3,3,3,5,5,7) or (3,3,5,5,5,5).

5 **Method 1.**
Let R = the remainder when 17 and 30 are divided by the required number N. If we subtract the remainder R from 17 and from 30, then N will divide the new numbers without remainder. In other words, 17 – R and 30 – R are multiples of N. N will also divide the sum (30 – R) + (17 – R) and the difference (30 – R) – (17 – R). But (30 – R) – (17 – R) = 30 – 17 = 13. Since N is to be as large as possible, N = 13. Observe that when each of 17 and 30 is divided by 13, the remainder is 4 in each case. Also observe that N is equal to the difference of the two given numbers. This will be true for a similar problem involving any two natural numbers.

Method 2.
Test various divisors in decreasing order until the remainders for 17 and 30 are the same. Then that divisor will be the largest which satisfies the given conditions.

Divisor	Remainder for 17	Remainder for 30
16	1	14
15	2	0
14	3	2
13	4	4

The number 13 is the largest number which divides 17 and 30 with the same remainder.

Olympiad 22

5 **Method 3.**
The following solution is advanced. If the algebra is too difficult for the reader, he or she is advised to skip what follows. Let D represent the divisor, Q_1 and Q_2 the quotients, and R the remainder.

$$\frac{30}{D} = Q_1 + \frac{R}{D} \quad \text{or} \quad 30 = Q_1D + R$$

$$\frac{17}{D} = Q_2 + \frac{R}{D} \quad \text{or} \quad 17 = Q_2D + R$$

By subtraction: $13 = Q_1D - Q_2D$ or $D(Q_1 - Q_2)$
Since D is a factor of 13, the largest value it may have is 13.

Olympiad 23

1 The average increase is 3. The average of the set of increased numbers is $18 + 3 = 21$.

2 **Method 1.**
Slice the stairs vertically into 3 congruent figures. Each slice contains $1 + 3 + 5 + 7 = 16$ cubes. Then there are $3 \times 16 = 48$ cubes.

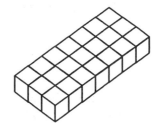

Method 2.
Slice the stairs into 4 horizontal layers. The bottom layer has 21 cubes, the next layer has 15, the next layer has 9, and the top layer has 3,

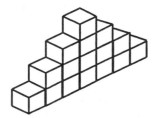

3 A number whose square is between 1,000 and 2,000 must be greater than 30 and less than 50 because $30 \times 30 = 900$ and $50 \times 50 = 2,500$. The smallest square between 1,000 and 2,000 is $32 \times 32 = 1024$; the largest square is $44 \times 44 = 1,936$. The square numbers are:
$$32 \times 32, \ 33 \times 33, \ 34 \times 34, \ \ldots \ , \ 44 \times 44; \quad \text{or} \quad 32^2, \ 33^2, \ 34^2, \ \ldots \ , \ 44^2$$
Therefore, there are 13 square numbers between 1000 and 2000.

Olympiad 23

4 Since each cycle has two wheels, there are 25 cycles on sale. If each of the cycles on sale was a bicycle, there would be just 50 wheels. An additional 14 wheels are needed to make the given total of 64 wheels. Therefore there must be 14 tricycles.

5 The weight of the water poured out was 10 – 5¾ = 4¼ lb. Since this is ½ of the total weight of the water, the total weight of the water must be 2 x 4¼ = 8½ lb. Then the jar weighs 10 – 8½ = 1½ or 1.5 lb.

Olympiad 24

1 A was 14 years old when B was born in 1962. Fourteen years later, A was 28 and B was 14. Therefore A was twice as old as B in 1976.

2 **Method 1.**
Let s = the length of one side of the square as shown. Then one of the congruent rectangles has perimeter:
$$s + \tfrac{1}{2}s + s + \tfrac{1}{2}s = 3s.$$
Since 3s = 18, s = 6 and 4s = 24.
Answer: The perimeter of the square is 24.

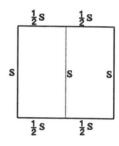

Method 2.
To avoid the use of fractions, let the length of each side of the square be 2s. Then the perimeter of one of the rectangles is 6s. Since 6s = 18, s = 3, and a side of the square is 2s = 6.

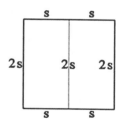

3

Since there is no remainder, the second partial product must end in 1. The only two digits whose product ends in 1 are 7 and 3. The sum of 7 and 3 is 10.

139

4 **Method 1.**
10 = 2 x 5
10,000 = (2x5) x (2x5) x (2x5) x (2x5)
10,000 = (2x2x2x2) x (5x5x5x5)   (by regrouping)
10,000 =   16   x   625

Method 2.
$10,000 = 10^4 = (2\times5)^4 = = 2^4 \times 5^4 = 16 \times 625$

5

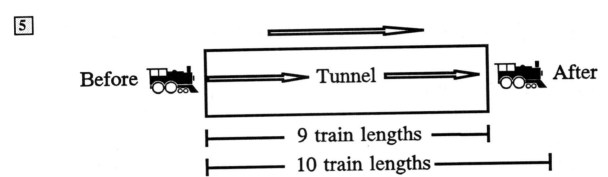

The train travels a distance equal to 10 times the train length (see diagram). The rate of 30 miles per hour is equivalent to 1/2 mile per minute. Since the train takes 2 minutes to clear the tunnel, it will travel a distance of 1 mile in 2 minutes. One mile also happens to be 10 times the train's length. Therefore the length of the train is 1/10 of a mile or 528 feet.

Olympiad 25

1 Numbers between 20 and 80 which are multiples of 7:

21, 28, 35, 42, 49, 56, 63, 70, 77

If 1 is added to the desired multiple of 7, the sum is a multiple of 5. Then the multiple of 7 must end in 4 or 9. Only 49 satisfies this condition. Therefore, 6 years from now I will be 49 + 6 = 55.

2 **Method 1.**
Represent the people by A, B, C, D, E, and F. Let AB represent a match between A and B. Then the set of different matches can be represented by:

$$
\begin{array}{lllll}
AB, & AC, & AD, & AE, & AF \\
BC, & BD, & BE, & BF, & \\
CD, & CE, & CF, & & \\
DE, & DF, & & & \\
EF & & & &
\end{array}
$$

There are 15 different matches listed above. Since each match occurs three times, there will be 45 matches in the tournament.

Method 2.
Make a diagram to show all possible pairings.

Each pairing is associated with a line segment joining two letters. There are 6x5 = 30 pairings. However each pairing is repeated. The pairing (B,F) also appears in the fifth diagram as (F,B). Therefore we need to divide 30, the number of pairings, by 2. Thus there are 15 different matches.

Comment: For a similar problem in a different setting, see Olympiad 38, problem 3, p. 58.

3 Since 20 x 20 x 20 = 8000 and 30 x 30 x 30 = 27,000, the three consecutive numbers are between 20 and 30. One of the three numbers must end in 5; otherwise the product cannot end in 0. Another number of the three must have a factor of 4; otherwise the product cannot end in 00. The possibilities are: 23, 24, 25 and 24, 25, 26. Since 23 x 24 x 25 = 13,800 and 24 x 25 x 26 = 15,600, the required numbers are 24, 25 and 26.

4 For the average to be 1, the sum of the three numbers must be 3.

$$
\text{Then} \quad \frac{1}{2} + \frac{1}{3} + ? = 3 \quad \text{or} \quad ? = 3 - \frac{5}{6} = 2\frac{1}{6} \quad \text{or} \quad \frac{13}{6}
$$

Olympiad 25

5 If A 5 5 B is divisible by 36, then it is also divisible by any factor of 36 and, in particular, by 4 and 9. The number formed by the last two digits, 5 B, must be divisible by 4.[3] Therefore B is either 2 or 6. A + 5 + 5 + B must be 18.[4] If B = 2, A = 6; if B = 6, A = 2. In either case, the sum A + B = 8.

Olympiad 26

1 **Method 1**
There are 31+22 = 53 days in the interval from Jan. 1 to Feb. 22 inclusive. Mondays occur on days #1, #8, #15, #22, #29, #36, #43, and #50 of the interval. Then day #53 is on Thursday.

Method 2
February 22 occurs 52 days after January 1. Mondays occur 7 days, 14 days, 21 days, . . . , and 49 days after January 1. Then 52 days after January 1 is Thursday.

2 If the blank interior spaces were covered by Xs, the entire figure would contain 8x18 = 144 Xs, the blank rectangular region would contain 3x5 = 15 Xs, and the blank triangular region would contain 1+3+5 = 9 Xs. Therefore, there are 144 – (9+15) = 120 Xs.

3 Only the following triples of natural numbers have a product of 24:
$$(1,1,24), (1,2,12), (1,3,8), (1,4,6), (2,2,6), (2,3,4).$$
Answer: There are six triples which each have a product of 24.

4 There are 12x8 = 96 individual daily rations. If the number of scouts is increased to 16, the 96 individual daily rations will last for 96 ÷ 16 = 6 days.

For similar problems in different settings, see Olympiad 1, problem 5, and Olympiad 7, problem 4.

5 Each of the required numbers will divide 171 – 6 = 165 without remainder. Since 165 = 3x5x11, the required divisors are:
$$11, 3x5, 3x11, \text{ and } 5x11, \text{ or } 11, 15, 33, \text{ and } 55.$$

---

[3] If a given number is divisble by 2^n, the number formed by the last n digits of the given number is divisible by 2^n.

[4] If a number is divisble by 9, its digit-sum is a multiple of 9.

Olympiad 27

1 The cost of any number of 5¢-stamps will have a units digit of 0 or 5. Therefore the cost of the 13¢-stamps must also have a units digit of 0 or 5. But 0 is not possible since there is no multiple of 13 less than 100 that has a units digit of 0. The only multiple of 13 less than 100 that has a units digit of 5 is 65. Therefore, Carol bought five 13¢-stamps for 65¢. The remaining 35¢ was spent for seven 5¢-stamps.[5]

2 If the area of the square is 144 square inches, the length of a side is 12 inches. Then each of the congruent rectangles is 4 inches by 6 inches. The required perimeter is 20.

3 Since the sum of A, B, and C in the units column ends in C, A + B = 10. In the tens column, the sum of A, B, C, and the carry of 1 (from the units column) ends in A. Then B + C + 1 = 10 and A + B + C + 1 is less than 20. Therefore the hundreds digit of the sum BAC is 1. Since B = 1, A = 9 and C = 8.

Answer: A = 9, B = 1, C = 8.

4 Since $40^2 = 1600$ and $50^2 = 2500$, the year is between 41^2 and 49^2. Since $43^2 = 1649$, $44^2 = 1936$, $45^2 = 2025$, the desired year is 1936.

5 **Method 1.**
Let T represent the tens digit and U the units digit. The difference condition may be expressed as

$$\begin{array}{r} T\ U \\ -\ U\ T \\ \hline 4\ 5 \end{array}$$

where T > U. The table at the right shows values that T and U may have to satisfy the above difference-condition. Then 94 is the largest two-digit number that satisfies the given conditions.

T	U
9	4
8	3
7	2
6	1

Method 2.
The largest value T may have is 9. Then the difference-condition can be expressed as shown at the right. In the units column, U must be 4. Therefore TU is 94.

$$\begin{array}{r} 9\ U \\ -\ U\ 9 \\ \hline 4\ 5 \end{array}$$

---

[5] A related problem can be seen in a different setting in Olympiad 16, problem 2.

Olympiad 28

1 The largest value occurs when A = 40 and B = 39; $\dfrac{40 \times 39}{40 - 39} = 1560$.

2 The clock must lose the equivalent of 12 hours or 720 minutes before it will again show the correct time. Since the clock loses 1 minute every hour, it will lose 720 minutes in 720 hours.

3 **Method 1.**
Since the number is divisible by 3 and 5, it is also divisible by 15. Examine multiples of 15: 15, 30, 45, 60, 75, 90, . . . Now find the smallest of these multiples which when divided by 7 will have a remainder of 4. That number is 60. (Other multiples of 15 which have this property are: 165, 270, 375, . . .)

Method 2.
The numbers which have a remainder of 4 when divided by 7 are:
$$4, 11, 18, 25, 32, 38, 46, 53, 60, 67, \ldots$$
The smallest of these numbers which is also divisible by 15 is 60.

Method 3. (Advanced)
Numbers which have a remainder of 4 when divided by 7 can be expressed as
$$7N + 4 \text{ where } N = 1, 2, 3, \ldots$$
Multiples of 15 can be expressed as
$$15M \text{ where } M = 1, 2, 3, \ldots$$

Given . . . . (1)	$7N + 4$	$= 15M$
Subtract 4 from both members . . . . . . (2)	$7N$	$= 15M - 4$
Divide both members by 7 . . . . (3)	N	$= \dfrac{15}{7}M - \dfrac{4}{7}$
	or N	$= 2\dfrac{1}{7}M - \dfrac{4}{7}$
Expand right member as shown . . . . . . (4)	N	$= 2M + \dfrac{1}{7}M - \dfrac{4}{7}$

Since N and 2M are whole numbers, then $\left[\dfrac{1}{7}M - \dfrac{4}{7}\right]$ is also a whole number. Then M may have the following values: 4, 11, 18, 25, . . . Test the smallest of these, 4. When M = 4, N = 8. Therefore the desired number is 60.

Olympiad 28

4 The top face of each cube which has 3 red faces is marked by a star. There are 16 stars and therefore 16 cubes which have 3 red faces.

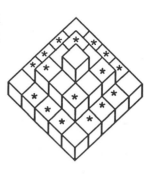

5 In 1 minute Alice can do $\frac{1}{60}$ of the job and Betty can do $\frac{1}{30}$ of the job.

Working together, they can do $\frac{1}{60} + \frac{1}{30} = \frac{3}{60}$ or $\frac{1}{20}$ of the job in one minute.

Then $\frac{20}{20}$ or the entire job will require 20 minutes.

Olympiad 29

1 The required multiples are:

    12, 15, 18, 21, . . . , 225, or 4x3, 5x3, 6x3, 7x3, . . . , 75x3

There are 72 multiples of 3 between 10 and 226.

2 **Method 1.**

Partition ABCD into congruent right triangles as shown. The rectangle contains 8 triangles; triangle EFG contains 2 triangles. Then triangle EFG has $\frac{2}{8}$ or $\frac{1}{4}$ of the total area, or $\frac{1}{4}$ of 36 = 9.

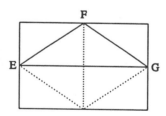

Method 2.

Assign any measures to the dimensions of the rectangle which will result in an area of 36. Suppose we let the length and width be 9 and 4 respectively. Then the area of the triangle will be ½ x 9 x 2 = 9.

See *Comment* next page.

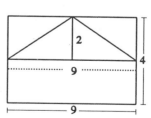

Olympiad 29

Comment: If we let the length and width of the rectangle be L and W respectively, the area of the triangle is ½ x L x ½W which is equivalent to ¼ (LxW). Therefore, the area of the triangle is always ¼ of the area of the rectangle, no matter what values are assigned to L and W.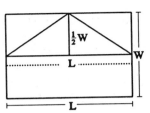

3 85 can be expressed as a product of two factors in two ways: 17x5 or 85x1. In each of the two ways, the larger factor represents the sum of the two whole numbers and the smaller factor represents the difference. Since the difference cannot be 1, 17 must be the sum.

4 The numbers which have 5 as a factor are: 5, 10, 15, 20, 25, 30. These numbers will give seven 5's. (Remember: 25 = 5x5).

5

Pages	Pieces of Type
1-9	9x1 = 9
10-99	90x2 = 180
100-150	51x3 = 153
	342 Total

Olympiad 30

1 From 1 to 1000, there are 100 groups of 10: 1-10, 11-20, 21-30, . . . , 991-1000. Each group of 10 contains just two numbers which end in 2 or 7. Therefore there are 100x2 = 200 numbers which end in 2 or 7. But the first group of 10 should not be included. Therefore, there are 200-2 = 198 numbers.

2 Each time 4 coins are taken out of the pocket, just one coin remains. Thus, there are 5 different coins that can be the one that remains. For each of the five coins that remains, there is the sum of the other four coins which is different from other sums. Therefore there are 5 possible sums.

Olympiad 30

[3] Front wheel makes $\frac{5280}{3}$ = 1760 turns. Rear wheel makes $\frac{5280}{4}$ = 1320 turns. Front wheel makes 1760 – 1320 = 440 more turns.

[4] The 9 in the first partial product is the units digit of the product CxC. Then C can be either 3 or 7. Suppose C = 3. The 4 in the second partial product is the units digit of the product 3xB. Then B = 8. Similarly the 1 in the third partial · product is the units digit of the product 3xA. Then A = 7.

Answer: A = 7, B = 8, C = 3.

If C = 7, it can be shown that B = 2 and A = 3. But the second and third partial products will then each have just three digits. Therefore C cannot be 7.

[5] Work backwards.

Condition	Anne	Betty	Total
1. End	12	12	24
2. Betty gave Ann as many cents as Ann had. (Ann must have had 6.)	6	18	24
3. Ann gave Betty as many cents as Betty had. (Betty must have had 9.)	15	9	24

Answer: Ann had 15¢

Olympiad 31

[1] 2/3 of the brick weighs 4 pounds. Then 1/3 of the brick weighs 2 pounds. It follows that 3/3 of the entire brick weighs 6 pounds.

[2] The "middle" number of any set of consecutive numbers also is the average of the set. Try this out on sets like: 5, 7, 9, and 8, 9, 10, 11, 12. (If the set has an even number of elements like: 9, 11, 13, 15, there is no "middle" number unless you consider it to be the number halfway between 11 and 13 which happens to be 12. The average of the set is 12.)

In our problem, 41 is the "middle" number: _ , _ , _ , 41 , _ , _ , _ . Counting backwards by 2s gives 35 as the first number.

3 **Method 1.**
Any number of the form ABA will be the same when the order of the digits is reversed. Clearly, A may be any digit but zero; B may any of the ten digits. Since there are nine choices for A and ten for B, there are 90 counting numbers which satisfy the given conditions.

Method 2.
A partial listing follows.

101	111	121	131	141	151	161	171	181	191
202	212	222	232	242	 292
.	.	.	.	.	.	.	.	.	.
.	.	.	.	.	.	.	.	.	.
909	919	929	939	949	 999

4 When the wheel makes one complete turn, it has rolled a distance of 88 inches. The number of turns equals 1 mile divided by 88 inches, or

$$\frac{5280 \times 12 \text{ inches}}{88 \text{ inches}} = 720$$

5 D in the sum DEER must be 1. The R in the second addend must be 9. It follows that E must be 0 and DEER represents 1009.

$$
\begin{array}{ccccc}
 & & & I & N \\
+ & R & I & D \\
\hline
D & E & E & R \\
\end{array}
$$

1 What number multiplied by 2½ gives 50 as an answer? This question is equivalent to: what number is equal to 50 divided by 2½? The number is 20. To get the correct answer, divide 20 by 2½. The correct answer is 8.

2 $40^2 = 1600$, $50^2 = 2500$. The number we seek is between 40 and 50. To get closer bounds on the number, try $45^2 = 2025$.

Since 2025 is "close" to 1985, try $44^2 = 1936$.

$$44^2 < 1985 < 45^2$$

44^2 differs from 1985 by 49; 45^2 differs from 1985 by 40.

Answer: The number whose square is closest to 1945 is 45.

3 **Method 1.**
From the first two sentences, we determine that Bill is 5 years older than Carl. From the third sentence, we know that the sum of the ages of Bill and Carl is 31. If we add 5 to both parts of the condition given by the third sentence, we get the sum of the ages of Bill and Carl plus 5 is 31 + 5. But Carl's age plus 5 is equal to Bill's age. So the modified third sentence can now be written as twice Bill's age is 36. It follows that Bill's age is 18. Then Carl's age is 13, and A's age from the first sentence is 7.

Answer: Bill is 18 years old and the oldest.

Method 2.
Let A, B, and C represent the respective ages of Al, Bill, and Carl.

Given . . . . (1)	A	+	B		= 25
Given . . . . (2)	A			+ C	= 20
Given . . . . (3)			B	+ C	= 31
Add the members of (1), (2), (3) . . . . . . (4)	2A	+	2B	+2C	= 76
Divide the members of (4) by 2 . . . . (5)	A	+	B	+ C	= 38
Subtract (1) from (5) . . . . (6)				C	= 13
Subtract (2) from (5) . . . . (7)			B		= 18
Subtract (3) from (5) . . . . (8)	A				= 7

Answer: Bill is 18 years old and the oldest.

4 Let 3S represent the length of a side of the square as shown in the diagram. Then the perimeter of one of the congruent rectangles is 8S or 16. It follows that S = 2, and 3S, the length of a side of the square, is 6. Therefore, the perimeter of the square is 24 meters.

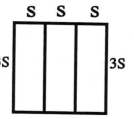

5 List the amounts using

1 coin: 1, 2, 4, 8

2 coins: 1+2, 1+4, 1+8, 2+4, 2+8, 4+8

3 coins: 1+2+4, 1+2+8, 1+4+8, 2+4+8

4 coins: 1+2+4+8

There are 15 different amounts that can be made. Notice that the amounts are the natural numbers from 1 to 15 inclusive.

1 **Method 1.**
If the weight of one bowl and the marbles it contains is 50 ounces, then the weight of two bowls and twice as many marbles is 100 ounces. It is given that the weight of one bowl and twice as many marbles is 92 ounces. Then the difference of weights between 100 ounces and 92 ounces is the weight of the bowl, or 8 ounces.

Method 2.
The increase in weight from 50 ounces to 92 ounces occurs because the weight of the marbles is doubled. That increase therefore is the weight of the original set of marbles, 42 ounces. It follows that the bowl weighs 8 ounces.

2 One less than the number is a multiple of 5 and also of 7, or of 35. then the number is 1 more than a multiple of 35: 36, 71, 106, 141, and so forth. The smallest odd number of this set is 71.

3 **Method 1.**
Count the number of cubes in each horizontal layer starting at the top.

No. of the layer	No. of cubes in the layer
1	1
2	3
3	6
4	10
5	15
Total	35

Method 2.
Count the number of cubes in each vertical column.

Column height	Number of Columns	Total No. of Cubes
5	1	5 x 1 = 5
4	2	4 x 2 = 8
3	3	3 x 3 = 9
2	4	2 x 4 = 8
1	5	1 x 5 = 5
	Total	35

Olympiad 33

4

		Time elapsed on slow clock (min)	Time elapsed on normal clock (min)
	(1)	45	60
Divide (1) by 3:	(2)	15	20
Add (1) and (2):	(3)	60	80

60 minutes on the slow clock is equivalent to 80 minutes on the normal clock.

Answer: The correct time will be 80 minutes after 9 or 10:20.

Comment: Another strategy would be to find what 1 minute on the slow clock is equivalent to on the normal clock. This is obtained by dividing each of 45 and 60 by 45. Then 45/45 or 1 minute on the slow clock is equivalent to 60/45 or 1⅓ minutes on the normal clock. Then 60 minutes on the slow clock is equivalent to 60 x 1⅓ or 80 minutes on the normal clock.

5 **Method 1.**

Let A = the number of marbles Anne has at the outset, and B = the number of marbles Betty has at the outset. Make a table of values for A and B at the outset using the information that B is 2 more than A. Make a second table showing what happens when Anne gives 1 marble to Betty.

Outset		Anne Gives 1 to Betty	
A	B	A−1	B+1
1	3	0	4
2	4	1	5
3	5	2	6
4	6	3	7
5	7	4	8

The second table shows that Betty will have twice as many if, at the outset, Anne had 5 and Betty had 7.

Method 2.

At the outset, let Betty have N+1 marbles and Anne N−1 marbles. When Anne gives Betty 1 marble, Betty will then have N+2 and Anne will have N−2. But Betty now has twice as many as Anne now has.

$$(1) \quad N + 2 = 2\times(N - 2) \text{ or } 2N - 4$$
$$(2) \quad 6 = N$$

Therefore Betty who had N+1 marbles actually had 7 marbles and Anne who had N−1 marbles actually had 5 marbles.

Olympiad 33

5 Method 3.

Use diagrams to show what happens.

At the outset, let Anne have N+1 marbles and Betty N+1+2 as shown. When Anne gives 1 to Betty, Anne then will have N and Betty will have N+1+2+1 or N+4.

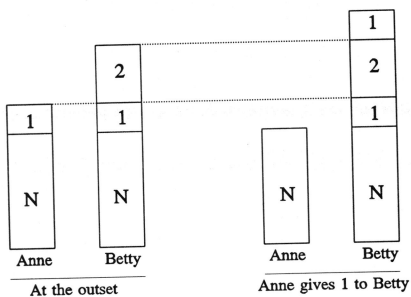

At the outset   **Anne gives 1 to Betty**

After Anne gives 1 marble to Betty, Anne has N marbles and Betty has N + 4 marbles. But what Betty now has is twice what Anne now has. Then N = 4. Therefore, at the outset, Anne had 5 marbles and Betty had 7 marbles.

Olympiad 34

1 Method 1.

$$\text{Given:} \quad 1 + 2 + 3 + 4 + \ldots + 25 = 325$$
$$\text{Find:} \quad 26 + 27 + 28 + 29 + \ldots + 50 = \quad ?$$

In the second series, each addend is 25 more than the corresponding addend of the first series which is located directly above. Since there are twenty-five addends in the second series, the sum of the second series is 25x25 or 625 greater than 325. The sum is 950.

Method 2.

Since the average of 1, 2, 3, 4, . . . , 25
is the "middle" number which is 13, then the average of
26, 27, 28, . . . , 50 is 13 + 25 or 38.
Then the sum of 26, 27, 28, . . . , 50 is 38 x 25 or 950.

Olympiad 34

1 **Method 3.**

The sum of the second series can be found without using the first series. Let S = the sum of the second series.

Given	(1)	S =	26 + 27 + 28 + ... + 49 + 50
Rewrite (1) in reverse order .	(2)	S =	50 + 49 + 48 + ... + 27 + 26
Add (1) and (2)	(3)	S =	76 + 76 + 76 + ... + 76 + 76

Since 76 appears
   as addend 25 times . . . . . . (4) 2S = 76 x 25
Divide both members by 2 . . (5) S = 38 x 25 or 950

2 Let N = the number of nickels, D = the number of dimes, and Q = the number of quarters that Eric has. Then:

$$Q < D \text{ and } N < Q, \text{ or } N < Q < D$$

If N = 2, then Q has to be at least 3 and D at least 4. But this will result in too many coins. Therefore N = 1. If Q = 3, then D has to be at least 4. Again this will result in too many coins. Therefore Q = 2. Since N = 1, D = 4 to bring the total number to 7. The total value of the coins is 95¢.

3 The length of a side of the square is 6m. Then the perimeter of rectangle AEFG is (3+12+3+12) or 30 meters.

4 **Method 1.**

In the first division, $\underline{b}$ is represented by 4. In the second division, $\underline{b}$ is represented by 5. $\underline{b}$ should have the same value in both divisions. This can be done by finding equivalent fractions for 3/4 and for 5/6 in which the replacements for 4 and 5 are the same. Since the LCM(4,5) = 20, replace

$$\frac{3}{4} \text{ with } \frac{3 \times 5}{4 \times 5} \text{ or } \frac{15}{20}, \text{ and } \frac{5}{6} \text{ with } \frac{5 \times 4}{6 \times 4} = \frac{20}{24}.$$

In the equivalent fractions, $\underline{a}$ = 15, $\underline{b}$ = 20, and $\underline{c}$ = 24. When $\underline{a}$ is divided by $\underline{c}$, the result is 15/24 or 5/8.

Method 2.

The given information can be represented as:

$$\frac{a}{b} = \frac{3}{4} \text{ and } \frac{b}{c} = \frac{5}{6}$$

If we multiply the members of both equations, we get:

$$\frac{a}{b} \times \frac{b}{c} = \frac{3}{4} \times \frac{5}{6}; \text{ or } \frac{a}{c} = \frac{5}{8}$$

5 Principle: If two numbers have the same remainder when divided by N, then their difference is a multiple of N. (Try it out.) The differences are:
$$539 - 414 = 125, \quad 539 - 364 = 175, \quad \text{and} \quad 414 - 364 = 50.$$
Each of the differences is divisible by N. Then N is the greatest common divisor of the differences: N = GCD(125, 175, 50). N = 25.

See Olympiad 22, problem 5 for a related problem.

Olympiad 35

1 Suppose as many schools as possible entered 4 teams. The multiple of 4 that is closest to and less than 347 is 344. In this case, it would take 86 schools to enter 344 teams. The remaining 3 teams could be entered by 1 school. Therefore the smallest number of schools that could enter 347 teams is 87.

2 $21 + 21 + 21 + 21 + 15 = 99$

3 **Method 1.**
$$\frac{1}{2 + \frac{1}{2}} + \frac{1}{3 + \frac{1}{3}} = \frac{1}{\frac{5}{2}} + \frac{1}{\frac{10}{3}}$$
$$= \frac{2}{5} + \frac{3}{10}$$
$$= \frac{7}{10}$$

Method 2. (suggested by a student)
$$\frac{1}{2\frac{1}{2}} = \frac{1 + 1}{2\frac{1}{2} + 2\frac{1}{2}} = \frac{2}{5}$$
$$\frac{1}{3\frac{1}{3}} = \frac{1 + 1 + 1}{3\frac{1}{3} + 3\frac{1}{3} + 3\frac{1}{3}} = \frac{3}{10}$$
$$\frac{2}{5} + \frac{3}{10} = \frac{4}{10} + \frac{3}{10} = \frac{7}{10}$$

Olympiad 35

4

	Number of new members
1st week	1
2nd week	2
3rd week	4
4th week	8
5th week	16
Total	31

5 **Method 1.**

The following graphs show the number of minutes after noon when the two lights flash. Noon is represented by 0 on the graphs.

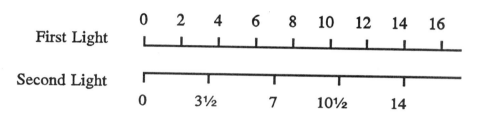

Both lights flash together every 14 minutes. Then both lights will flash together 5x14 or 70 minutes after noon or 1:10 P.M.

Method 2.

Since both lights flash together every 14 minutes, they will flash together at:
noon, 12:14, 12:28, 12:42, 12:56, 1:10, 1:24, 1:38, . . .
The first time after 1 P.M. that the lights will flash together will be 1:10 P.M.

Olympiad 36

1 It is clear that B = 0. If A is greater than 1, the difference of the 3-digit and the 2-digit numbers will be greater than 100. But the difference is given as a 2-digit number. Therefore A = 1. If we now replace A and B in the subtraction as shown at the right, it is clear that C must be 9.

$$\begin{array}{r} 1\ 0\ 1 \\ -\ C\ 1 \\ \hline 1\ 0 \end{array}$$

2 The "steps" have 4 vertical segments. The sum of the lengths of these 4 segments is equivalent to the length of side AD. In a similar way, we can show that the sum of the lengths of the 4 horizontal segments of the "steps" is equivalent to the length of side AB. Therefore the perimeter of the step-like figure is the same as the perimeter of the square ABCD -- 36 cm.

Olympiad 36

3 Since 10x10x10 = 1000 and 20x20x20 = 8000, the number we seek is between 10 and 20. Now consider the following products:

11x11x11, 12x12x12, 13x13x13, . . . , 19x19x19

Of these nine products, only 17x17x17 ends in 3. When the multiplication is done, we get 17x17x17 = 4913.

4 Let A be the point-score of the A-ring, and B the point-score of the inner circle. Then:

(1) 2A and 1B gives 17 points

(2) 1A and 2B gives 22 points.

Method 1.
Clearly, B's value is 5 more than A's value by comparing (1) and (2). Make a table of values for A and B in which B's value is 5 more than A's value. Then check to see if (1) is true: 2A and 1B gives 17 points.

A	B	2A + 1B
1	6	8
2	7	11
3	8	14
*4	9	17

*When A = 4 and B = 9, 2A + 1B = 17.

Method 2.
Add (1) and (2) . . . . (3) $3A + 3B = 39$
Divide both members of (3) by 3 . . . . (4) $A + B = 13$
Compare (4) with (2) . . . . (2) $A + 2B = 22$
Subtract (4) from (2) . . . . (5) $B = 9$

The value of B is 9 points.

5 The ones column of the 30 numbers contains 30 ones. Therefore its sum is 30; the ones digit of the sum is 0, carry 3. The tens column contains 29 ones. Therefore its sum is 29, carry 3, or 32. The tens digit of the sum is 2.

Olympiad 37

1

Boxes:	Large	Small	Smaller	Total
Number:	4	12	24	40

2 The number of coins is a multiple of 30: 30, 60, 90, 120, 150, . . . The smallest of these multiples which has a remainder of 1 when divided by 7 is 120.

Olympiad 37

3 **Method 1.**
There are 3 choices for the first move starting from A. Having made the first move, then there are 2 choices for the second move. Then there is just 1 choice for the third move. There are 3 x 2 x 1 or 6 paths from A to B.

Method 2.
Make diagrams of the different paths.

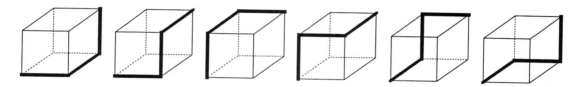

4 **Method 1.**
List the numbers.

					How many numbers
10					1
20	21				2
30	31	32			3
.					.
.					.
.					.
90	91	92	. . .	98	9
			Total		45

Method 2.
Consider the numbers: 01, 02, 03, . . . , 99. Of these 99 numbers, 9 have repeated digits: 11, 22, 33, . . . , 99. Then there are 90 two-digit numbers whose digits are not repeated. Half of these have a tens digit greater than the units digit.

5 **Method 1.**
Alice runs 50m while Betty runs 40m. Thus Alice runs 5m for every 4m Betty runs. In the 60m race, Alice runs 12 x 5m, and Betty runs 12 x 4 or 48m. Alice wins by 12m.

Method 2.
Since Alice wins the 50m race by 10, Alice must gain 2m over Betty for every 10m that Alice runs. In a 60m race, Alice gains 6 x 2m or 12m.

Olympiad 38

1 The largest value of the sum occurs when 3 and 5 are assigned to B and C.

$$\begin{array}{r} 3\,2\,5 \\ +\ 5\,2\,3 \\ \hline 8\,4\,8 \end{array}$$

2 $(5273)^6$ and $(3)^6$ have the same units digit.

Method 1.

Number	3^2	3^3	3^4	3^5	3^6
Units digit	9	7	1	3	9

Answer: 9

Method 2.

$$3^6 = 3^2 \times 3^4 = 9 \times 81 = 729$$

The units digit of $(5273)^6$ is 9.

3 Suppose each team played just one game with each of the remaining teams. Then each of the nine teams plays 8 games. This makes a total of 9x8 or 72 games. But each game has been counted twice in this total. For example, the game between Team A and Team B appears in A's 8 games and also B's 8 games. Therefore there are 9x8/2 = 36 different games played. Since each game is played three times, the total number of games played is 108.

Comment: For a similar problem in a different setting, see Olympiad 25, Problem 2, p. 45. Also see the solution, p. 141.

4 If June 1 is a Sunday, so are June 8, 15, 22, and 29. But that gives five Sundays in the month. Therefore June 1 and June 29 cannot be Sundays, and June 30 cannot be a Monday. Similarly, if June 2 is a Sunday, so are June 9, 16, 23, and 30. Again, this gives five Sundays. Therefore June 30 cannot be a Sunday.

5 **Method 1.**

No. of red faces	No. of one-inch cubes
*3	8
*2	12
1	6
0	1
Total No.	27

* Number of cubes with 2 or 3 red faces is 8 + 12 = 20.

Method 2.
The square in the center of each face is the outside face of a one-inch cube having just one red face. There are six such cubes, one for each face. There is one cube in the center of the three-inch cube which does not have paint on any face. All the other cubes have paint on two or three faces. Their number is 27 – (6 + 1) = 20.

Olympiad 39

1 | Statement | Possible order of digits |
"3" is next to "8"	38 or 83
"2" is not next to "3"	382, 283, 38_2, or 2_83
"5" is not next to "2"	5382 or 2835

Since the number is less than 5000, the answer is 2835.

2 **Method 1.**

Six apples cost 50¢ and sell for 75¢. Thus a profit of 25¢ is made on a sale of 6 apples. If four such sales are made, a profit of 4x25¢ or $1 will result.

Method 2.

The profit on one apple = $\dfrac{25}{2} - \dfrac{25}{3} = \dfrac{25}{6}$

$$\frac{\text{Total Profit}}{\text{Profit per apple}} = \text{Number of apples}$$

$$100 \div \frac{25}{6} \text{ per apple} = 24 \text{ apples}$$

3 **Method 1:**

Rotate region I about point D (see figure 2) until it falls in place as shown in figure 3.

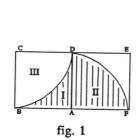 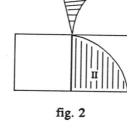 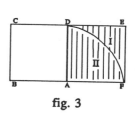

fig. 1   fig. 2   fig. 3

Area I + Area II = Area square ADEF.

Note: This "neat" method was found in the notebooks of Leonardo DaVinci.

Method 2.
Area II = Area III.
Therefore Area I + Area II = Area I + Area III = Area ADEF

4 **Method 1.**
Consider fractions equivalent to $\frac{2}{3}$: $\frac{4}{6}$, $\frac{6}{9}$, $\frac{8}{12}$, $\frac{10}{15}$, $\cdots$

Of these fractions, $\frac{6}{9} = \frac{2+4}{5+4}$.   Therefore 4 is the number.

Method 2.
Test different whole numbers as addends.

$$\frac{2+1}{5+1} = \frac{3}{6}; \quad \frac{2+2}{5+2} = \frac{4}{7}; \quad \frac{2+4}{5+4} = \frac{6}{9}$$

Method 3.
Let N be the number that is added to the numerator and to the denominator.

Given . . . . (1) $\frac{2+N}{5+N} = \frac{2}{3}$

Multiply both members of (1) by 3(5 + N) . . (2) $3(2+N) = 2(5+N)$

or $6 + 3N = 10 + 2N$

Subtract 2N from both members . . . . (3) $6 + N = 10$

Subtract 6 from both members . . . . (4) $N = 4$

Therefore the number that should be added to the numerator and denominator of $\frac{2}{5}$ is 4. This will give the new fraction $\frac{6}{9}$ which is equivalent to $\frac{2}{3}$.

5 **Method 1.**
Make a table of ages for the three children beginning with the youngest and then the oldest.

Youngest	Oldest	Middle	Sum of the ages
5	10	7	22
6	12	9	27
*7	14	11	*32

The third line of the table satisfies the conditions of the problem. Therefore the age of the youngest child is 7.

Method 2.
Let Y = the age of the youngest. Then the age of the oldest is 2Y, and the age of the middle child is 2Y – 3.

Given . . . . (1) $Y+2Y+(2Y-3) = 32$

Simplify the left member . . . . (2) $5Y - 3 = 32$

Add 3 to both members . . . . (3) $5Y = 35$

Divide both members by 5 . . . . (4) $Y = 7$

The youngest child is 7.

Olympiad 40

1 There are 13 hours between 9 A.M. and 10 P.M. Thus the slow clock will lose 13 x 3 or 39 minutes and show 9:21 or 21:21 on a 24-hour clock.

2 The sum of the 4 entries on the major diagonal is 34. Then the missing entry at the bottom of the third column should be 2. Now calculate B; B = 13. Now calculate A; A + 4 + 16 + 13 = 34 or A + 33 = 34.

Answer: A = 1, B = 13.

3 Suppose XY represents the original two-digit number. Then Y must be 1 and X must be 4. Original number is 41.

$$\begin{array}{ccc} X & Y & 3 \\ - & X & Y \\ \hline 3 & 7 & 2 \end{array}$$

4 **Method 1.**

Area trapezoid = Area triangle ABC – Area triangle EBF

$$\text{Area } \Delta ABC = \frac{1}{2} \times 4 \times 4 = 8$$

$$\text{Area } \Delta EBF = \frac{1}{2} \times 2 \times 2 = 2$$

$$\text{Area } AEFC = 8 - 2 = 6$$

Method 2.
Let G be the midpoint of AC. Draw EG and GF.
Then ΔABC is divided into four small congruent triangles.
Since area ΔABC = 8, each small triangle has area 2.
Trapezoid AEFC has area 3x2 or 6.

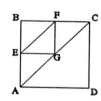

5 When Peter worked 3 fewer weeks than the agreed period of 8 weeks, he received $60 less than the original amount. Therefore each week's work was worth $20. At this rate, he was entitled to $160 for 8 weeks. Since he was to receive $85 and a bicycle, the latter was worth $75

Olympiad 41

1 The time 2 o'clock is repeated every 12 hours. There are 83 12s in 1000 plus a remainder of 4. Therefore the time will be 6 o'clock.

2 The sum of the five numbers is 5x6 = 30. After the number is removed, the sum of the remaining numbers is 4x7 = 28. The number that was removed is 2.

3

Order of terms	1	2	3	. . .	?
Terms of sequence	3	10	17	. . .	528
Multiples of 7	7	14	21	. . .	

Compare each term of the sequence with its corresponding multiple of 7. Notice that each multiple of 7 is 4 more than the corresponding term. The multiple of 7 that corresponds to 528 is 528 + 4 = 532. Since 532 = 7x76, 528 is the 76th term of the sequence.

4 10,000 = 100 x 100.

Each of the perfect squares 1x1, 2x2, 3x3, . . . , 99x99 is less than 100x100. Answer: There are 99 numbers in the above sequence.

5 **Method 1.**
Suppose just 2 people were seated at each of the 30 tables. Then a total of 60 people would be seated. Since the seating capacity is 81, there are 21 vacant seats. Each of the tables for 5 people has 3 vacant seats. There must be 7 tables which seat 5 people. Then there must be 23 tables which seat 2 people.

Method 2.
Make a table and look for a pattern.

Number of tables for 2	Number of tables for 5	Total number of people seated
30	0	60
29	1	63 = 60 + 1x3
28	2	66 = 60 + 2x3
. . .	. . .	. . . .
	7	81 = 60 + 7x3

In the right column; observe that the number of 3s added to 60 is the same as the number of tables for 5. Since 81 = 60 + 7x3, there must be 7 tables for 5 people and 23 tables for 2 people.

Method 3. Algebra
Let T denote the number of tables for 2 and F the number of tables for 5. Then: $T + F = 30$
          $2T + 5F = 81$

See *Solutions*, Olympiad 1, Problem 4, Method 3, p. 100.

Solutions

1 Since $8.00 \div 6 = \$1.33^{+}$, the most a book could cost is $1.33.

Since $8.00 \div 7 = \$1.14^{+}$, the least a book could cost is $1.15.

Notice that the first condition is not needed for the answer.

2

Numbers	Digit-sum
1– 9: 1, 2, 3, 4, . . . , 9	45
10–19: 10, 11, 12, 13, . . . , 19	45 (sum of units digits) 10 (sum of tens digits}
20–25: 20, 21, 22, 23, 24, 25	15 (sum of units digits) 12 (sum of tens digits)

Total   127

3 **Method 1.**

The average amount earned was $65/5 = \$13$ which also happens to be the amount earned for the third day. (Note: the third number of any five consecutive (also even or odd) numbers is the average of the five numbers). Therefore she earned $9 the first day.

Method 2.

Let F represent how much she earned the first day:

Day	1	2	3	4	5
Earnings	F	F+2	F+4	F+6	F+8

Alice's total earnings was $5F+20$ or five times what she earned the first day plus $20. If we subtract $20 from the total earned, the remainder $45 represents five times what she earned the first day. Then she earned $45/5 = \$9$ the first day.

4 There are 13 small squares in the figure, each with an area of 52/13 or 4 square units. Then each side of a small square has length of 2 units. Since there are 20 sides in the perimeter, the perimeter is 20x2 units or 40 units.

5 Four people working 15 days is equivalent to one person working 60 days. To complete the other half of the job, ten people would have to work 6 days which is also equivalent to one person working 60 days.

Olympiad 43

1 Each register had $150 after the transfer. Then, before the transfer, one register had 150 + 15, the other had 150 – 15. The larger amount was **$165**.

2 **Method 1.**
List pairs of factors of 128 and their quotient.

Factors	128 1	64 2	32 4	16 8
Quotient	128	32	8	2

Answer: The two numbers are 4 and 32

Method 2. Algebra
One number must be 8 times the other. Call the numbers B and 8B. Then 8B×B = 128. So B×B = 16, and B = 4. The other number is 8B, or 32.

3 There are many ways to partition the region. Here are two.

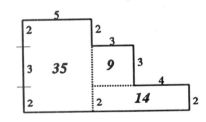 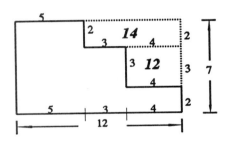

By addition:
   Area = 35 + 9 + 14 = 58

By subtraction:
   Area = 7 x 12 – 14 – 12 = 58

4 H must be 1. In order to get the carry from the tens column to the hundreds column, A must be 9. Then E = 0. HEE = 100.

5 **Method 1.**
To gain 30¢ in the exchange, the number of nickels (N) must be 6 more than the number of dimes (D). Since N is greater than D and N + D = 20, make a table for N and D beginning with N = 11. We seek a pair of values where N – D = 6.

N	11	12	13
D	9	8	7
N–D	2	4	6*

Answer: To begin with, Barbara had seven dimes.

Method 2. Algebra   N + D = 20
                               N – D = 6

See *Solutions,* Olympiad 16, Problem 2, Method 3, p. 128.

Olympiad 44

1 List multiples of 7 greater than 24 and less than 72. Also list the multiple of 6 which is less than and closest to the multiple of 7.

Multiples of 7:	28	35	42	49	56	63	70
Multiples of 6:	24	30	36	48	54	60	66

56 is the desired multiple of 7 which is 2 more than a multiple of 6.

Answer: My height is 56 inches.

2 **Method 1.**
BBB is divisible by 111 which equals 3x37. Then AB is either 37 or a multiple of 37 which, in this case, can only be 74. Test 37x6. It fails the given conditions. But 74x6 = 444 satisfies the given conditions.

Answer: AB is 74.

Method 2.
AB x 6 is an even number. Therefore B = 2, 4, 6, 8. Test each of these values for B in the given problem. Only 4 works.

3 **Method 1.** (Work backwards)

	had	**spent 1/3**	**left 2/3**	
store 1:	27 ——	9 ——	18	
store 2:	18 ——	6 ——	12 ——	Start here

Method 2.
Tom spent 1/3 of his money in store 1 and had 2/3 left. In store 2 he spent 1/3 of 2/3 of his original amount. In both stores he spent 1/3 + 1/3 x 2/3, or 3/9 + 2/9 = 5/9 of his money. Clearly he had 4/9 of his money left which was equal to $12. Then 1/9 of his money was $3. He originally had 9 x 3 or $27.

4 In the front view, all shaded cubes have 3 red faces. However there is one cube with 3 red faces that is not visible. See bottom view for this cube.

Answer: There are eleven cubes which each have red paint on just three faces.

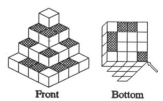

Front   Bottom

5 Since the number is divisible by 8 which equals 2x2x2 or 2^3, the number formed by the last three digits of the given number (43B) is divisible by 8. Digit B must be 2.

Since A95432 is divisible by 11, the difference between the sum of its odd-place digits and the sum of its even-place digits is 0 or a multiple of 11. In this case, the difference is 0. Then (A+5+3) – (9+4+2) = 0. This is equivalent to A = 7.

The above theorems on divisibility are discussed in <u>Creative Problem Solving in School Mathematics</u>, pp 98-99, 102-103.

Olympiad 45

1 OC = 8, OCTA = 8x8 = 64, OCTIL = 8x64 = 512, OCTILLA = 8x512 = 4096.

2 Since the sum of the three numbers in each diagonal is the same, and since they have the same middle number, the sum of each pair of numbers in opposite corners must be the same: 9 + 13 = 5 + ?. Clearly ? = 17. The bottom row now has a sum of 33. The middle number must be 11.

3 **Method 1.**
Since the number of FGs is 6 more than the number of FSs, subtract 12 points for 6 FGs from the total points: 72 – 12 = 60. Then 60 points represent the total points for equal numbers of FGs and FSs. One FG and one FS have a total point value of 3. Twenty FGs and twenty FSs have a total point value of 60. Then there must be twenty FSs and twenty-six FGs.

Method 2.
Make a table and look for a pattern.

FG	FS	Total Points	
6	0	12	Notice that the number of
7	$\boxed{1}$	15 = 12 + $\boxed{1}$ x 3	3s added to 12 in the
8	$\boxed{2}$	18 = 12 + $\boxed{2}$ x 3	total points column is the
. . .	. . .	. . . .	same as the number in the
	$\boxed{?}$	72 = 12 + $\boxed{20}$ = 3	FS column.

4 Each of the four congruent rectangles has a perimeter equivalent to 2½ sides of the square (s + s + $\frac{1}{4}$s + $\frac{1}{4}$s). Since the length of 2½ sides = 25 units, then, by doubling, we get the length of 5 sides = 50 units. Obviously, the length of one side is 10 units, and the perimeter of the square is 40 units.

5 **Method 1.**
Notice that each term of the second series is 4 times as large as the corresponding term of the first series.

$$1 \quad + \quad 4 \quad + \quad 9 \quad . . . \quad + \quad 625$$
$$4 \quad + \quad 16 \quad + \quad 36 \quad . . . \quad + \quad 2500$$
$$4 + 16 + 36 + . . . + 2500 = 4 \text{ x } (1 + 4 + 9 + . . . + 625) = 4 \text{ x } 5525 = 22,100$$

[5] **Method 2.**

The base of each term of the second series is an even number. The terms of the series can be represented:

$$(2x1)^2 + (2x2)^2 + (2x3)^2 + \ldots + (2x25)^2$$
$$\text{or} \quad 2^2x1^2 + 2^2x2^2 + 2^2x3^2 + \ldots + 2^2x25^2$$
$$\text{or} \quad 4x1^2 + 4x2^2 + 4x3^2 + \ldots + 4x25^2$$
$$\text{or} \quad 4x(1^2 + 2^2 + 3^2 + \ldots + 25^2) = 4 \times 5525 = 22,100$$

Note: $(2x3)^2 = 2^2x3^2$ because $(2x3)^2 = (2x3)(2x3)$ by definition

By rearranging factors, $(2x3)^2 = (2x2)(3x3) = 2^2x3^2$

[1] The largest amount that can be made is 49¢. Using the given set of coins, any amount from 1¢ to 49¢ can be made. Therefore there are 49 different amounts that can be made.

[2] **Method 1.**
Suppose the 30 people consisted solely of children. Then they would have paid 30x\$2 or \$60 for their tickets. Since \$87 was paid for the 30 tickets, the difference of \$27 was paid by adults. Each adult paid \$3 more than a child. There must have been 27/3 = 9 adults.

Method 2.
Make a table. Let C = number of children; A = number of adults. In the cost column, observe that the number of 3s added to 60 is the same number that appears in the A column. Since 87 = 60 + 9x3, there must be 9 adults in the group.

C	A	Cost of Tickets
30	0	60
29	1	63 = 60 + 1x3
28	2	66 = 60 + 2x3
27	3	69 = 60 + 3x3
·	·	. . . . . .
☐		87 = 60 + 9x3

Method 3. Algebra
$$C + A = 30$$
$$2C + 5A = 87$$

See *Solutions,* Olympiad 1, Problem 4, Method 3, p. 100.

Solutions

Olympiad 46

3

Method 1. Determine the number of cubes in each layer from the top layer down.

Layer	Number of Cubes
1	1x2 = 2
2	2x3 = 6
3	3x4 = 12
4	4x5 = 20
5	5x6 = 30
	Total = 70

Method 2. Add the number of visible cubes in each layer to the number of cubes in the preceding layer.

Layer	Number of Cubes	
1	2	= 2
2	2+4	= 6
3	2+4+6	= 12
4	2+4+6+8	= 20
5	2+4+6+8+10	= 30
	Total	= 70

Method 3.

Each of the visible cubes is at the top of a column of cubes. For example, each of the top two cubes of the tower is the top of a column of five cubes, and each of the four visible cubes in the next layer is the top of a column of four cubes. The following table shows the number of cubes in the columns of different sizes.

# of cubes in column	# of columns	# of cubes
5	2	10
4	4	16
3	6	18
2	8	16
1	10	10
	Total	70

4 If the average of five numbers is 16, the sum of the numbers is 80. When the sixth number, 10, is added to the five numbers, the sum of the six numbers is 90. The average of the six numbers is 90/6 = 15.

5

```
                          7   C ·   quotient
  divisor    A  B  / _  _  _  _
                   _  _  _      fpp
              _  _  _
              _  2  _         spp
              _  _  _
                     0
```

i)   AB must be less than 15 because ABx7 is the first partial product (fpp) which is a two-digit number.

ii) The greatest value that C could have is 9. Since ABxC is the second partial product (spp) which is a three-digit number, AB must be greater than 11.

iii) Clearly AB is between 11 and 15, or is 12, 13 or 14.

iv) When AB = 14 and C = 9, the tens digit of the spp will be 2.

v)   The other possibilities, AB = 12 or 13 and C = 8 or 9, will not yield a tens digit of 2 in the spp. Therefore A = 1, B = 4, and C = 9.

1 The cost of 12 cans at the old rate was 4x$2 or $8. The cost of 12 cans at the new rate was 3x$2.50 or $7.50. The new price is $.50 less than the old price.

2 Method 1.
condition a: 40 < N < 80
condition b: N could be 42, 47, 52, 57, 62, 67, 72, 77
condition c: N could be 46, 53, 60, 67, 74
The number that satisfies all three conditions is 67.

Method 2.
N must end in 2 or 7. Begin with 6x7 + 4 = 46 and count by 7's to the first number ending in 2 or 7. That number is 67.

3 Method 1.
The average of the five consecutive numbers is 100/5 or 20 which also happens to be the middle number. The smallest of the five consecutive numnbers is 18.

Method 2.
Let the five consecutive numbers be N, N+1, N+2, N+3, and N+4. The sum of the five numbers is 5N + 10.

Given . . . . (1) 5N + 10 = 100

Subtract 10 from both members of (1) . . . . . (2)   5N = 90

Divide both members of (2) by 5 . . . . (3)   N = 18

4 Method 1.
For each 4 steps the cat takes, the dog takes 3. Therefore when the cat takes 12 steps, the dog takes 9 steps which covers a distance of 9 feet. Therefore the cat covers 9 feet.

Method 2.
For each 4 steps the cat takes, the dog takes 3 which covers 3 feet. Therefore, 12 steps of the cat covers 3x3 feet or 9 feet.

5 i) S must be 3 or 8.
  ii) Since there must be a carry of 1 from the 100s column, H = 9 and E = 0. Then I = 5.
  iii) If S = 8, the carry of 1 to the tens column would make E an odd number. But this is impossible because E = 0. Therefore, S = 3. Place the known numbers in the example.

```
  T 9 5 3
+     5 3
---------
  K 0 0 6
```

  iv) T cannot be 1, 3, 5, 6, 9. If T = 2, K = 3. But S = 3. If T = 4, K = 5. But I = 5. If T = 7, K = 8. This does not violate any of the given conditions.
  Answer: THIS represents 7953.

1 List the triples so that the numbers in each triple are arranged according to size to prevent duplication. (1,1,8),(1,2,7),(1,3,6),(1,4,5),(2,2,6),(2,3,5,),(2,4,4),(3,3,4).

Answer: There are eight triples which each have a sum of 10.

2 **Method 1.**
If we add $12 to what Rhoda has, she will have as much as Patricia. If we add $15 to what Sarah has, she will also have as much as Patricia. Since all three have $87, then $87 + $12 + $15 or $114 represents three times what Patricia has. Then Patricia has $114/3 or $38.

Method 2.
Let P, R, S represent the amounts each of the people has.

Given . . . . (1) $P = R + 12$

Given . . . . (2) $P = S + 15$

Given . . . . (3) $P + R + S = 87$

Add 12 and 15 to
     both members of (3) . . . (4) $P + R + 12 + S + 15 = 87 + 12 + 15$

Substitute from (1) and (2)
     into (4) . . . . (5) $P + P + P = 114$

Divide both members by 3 . . (6) $P = 38$

3 **Method 1.** Let S be the sum of the numbers from 1 to 12.

Given . . . . (1) $S = 1 + 2 + 3 + \ldots + 12$

Reverse the order of . . . . (2) $S = 12 + 11 + 10 + \ldots + 1$
terms of the sum

Add (1) and (2) . . . . (3) $2S = 3 + 13 + 13 + \ldots + 13$

Simplify (3) . . . . (4) $2S = 12 \times 13$

Divide both sides by 2 . . . . (5) $S = 6 \times 13$ or 78

Method 2.
Arrange the 12 numbers which represent the number of squares in each column as follows:

1	2	3	4	5	6
12	11	10	9	8	7

Notice that the sum of each vertical pair is 13.

Answer: The sum of all 6 pairs is 6x13 = 78.

Olympiad 48

3 Method 3. (Somewhat impractical but good for class discussion.) Extend the given staircase until it is 12 units tall. Notice that it contains 3 of the original staircases 4 units tall and also 3 4x4 squares. Then the number of unit squares contained is 3x10 + 3x16 = 78.

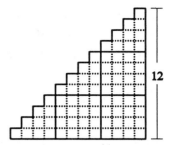

4 Method 1.

numbers:		8		17					?
order:	1	2	3	4	5	6	7	8	9	10

It takes 3 uniform increases to get from 8 to 17. Since the difference of 8 and 17 is 9, each increase must be 3. It takes 5 increases of 3 to get from 17 to the 10th number. The 10th number must be 17+15 or 32.

Method 2.
Let the difference between successive' numbers be D. Then the numbers that follow 8 are 8+D, 8+2D, and 8+3D. But 8+3D = 17. Then 3D is 9 and D is 3. The 10th number is 15 more than the 5th number; 17 + 15 = 32.

5 List some of the possible share values and the corresponding number of members (M) for each share value.

Share ($):	1	2	3	4	5	6	8	10	12	15	16
M:	240	120	80	60	48	40	30	24	20	16	15

Examine the table for a place where the value of a share increases by $1 as M decreases by 1. That occurs when the value of the original share is $15 for 16 members. Notice that the value of a share becomes $16 when there is 1 less member, or when there are 15 members. Therefore 15 members got a share of the $240.

Olympiad 49

1 If the number is divisible by both 7 and 8, it is also divisible by 56. Divide 56 into 999, the largest three-digit number as shown at the right. Then 999 – 47 = 952 (or 56 x 17 = 952) is the required number.

```
      1 7
56 / 9 9 9
    5 6
    -----
    4 3 9
    3 9 2
    -----
      4 7
```

Olympiad 49

2 **Method 1.**

The semiperimeter of the rectangle is 12 meters. Use a table to show some possible dimensions in meters and the corresponding areas in square meters.

dimension 1:	1	2	3	4	5	6
dimension 2:	11	10	9	8	7	6
area:	11	20	27	32	35	36

According to the dimensions shown, the largest area is 36. See Method 2 for a convincing demonstration that 36 is the largest area no matter what dimensions are chosen for the given rectangle.

Method 2.

If one dimension of the rectangle is more than 6, say 6+x, the other dimension must be 6-x. Otherwise the semiperimeter will not be 12. Compare the 6 by 6 square in fig. 1 with the (6+x) by (6-x) rectangle in fig. 2.

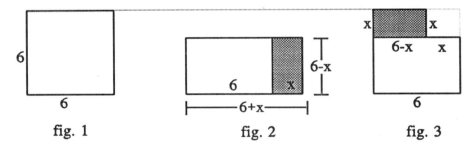

fig. 1   fig. 2   fig. 3

In fig 3, the shaded area of fig. 2 is moved to a new position. Now compare the area in fig. 3 with fig. 1. Notice that the difference in areas is equal to the area of the small missing square in the upper right corner of fig. 3. The area of the small missing square in fig. 3 is x·x. Therefore the area of fig. 2 is 36−x·x which is always smaller than 36, the area of the square. Therefore, for a given perimeter, the rectangle of largest area is a square.

3 **Method 1.**

1/3 of the number is the same as decreasing the number by 2/3 of itself. Then 2/3 of the number must be 8. It follows that 1/3 of the number must be 4. Then the number must be 12.

Olympiad 49

3 **Method 2.**
The diagram at the right shows that N/3 is obtained by subtracting 2/3 of N or 8 from N itself. If 8 is the value of 2 of the three boxes, then each box has value 4. N must be 12.

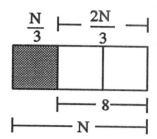

4

$$\text{Total Charge: } \$3.45$$
$$\text{Charge for first five pounds: } \underline{\$1.65}$$
$$\text{Charge for remaining pounds: } \overline{\$1.80}$$

Since the charge for each of the remaining pounds is 12¢ per pound, the number of remaining pounds is $180/12 = 15$. The total number of pounds in the package is $15 + 5$ or 20.

5 **Method 1.**
(Traditional Method) Change each fraction to a decimal equivalent.

$$\frac{1}{2} = 2\overline{)1.0}\;{}^{.5}; \quad \frac{.1}{2} = 2\overline{).10}\;{}^{.05}; \quad \frac{1}{.2} = .2\overline{)1.0}\;{}^{5} \; ; \quad A.BC = 5.55$$

Method 2.
Find equivalent fractions which do not have a decimal point. (This method is cumbersome, but it will work.)

$$\frac{1}{2}; \quad \frac{.1}{2} = \frac{.1 \times 10}{2 \times 10} = \frac{1}{20}; \quad \frac{1}{.2} = \frac{1 \times 10}{.2 \times 10} = \frac{10}{2}$$

$$\frac{1}{2} + \frac{1}{20} + \frac{10}{2} = \frac{10}{20} + \frac{1}{20} + \frac{100}{20} = \frac{111}{20} = 20\overline{)111.00}\;{}^{5.55}$$

Method 3. (Shortcut)
Multiplying a number by .1 results in moving the number's decimal point one place to the left. Dividing a number by .1 results in moving the number's decimal point one place to the right.

Begin with $\dfrac{1}{2} = .5; \quad \dfrac{.1}{2} = .1 \times \dfrac{1}{2} = .1 \times .5 = .05; \quad \dfrac{1}{.2} = \dfrac{1}{.1 \times 2} = \dfrac{1/2}{.1} = \dfrac{.5}{.1} = 5$

Add the three equivalents: $.5 + .05 + 5 = 5.55$

1 The following symbols have the same meaning in the USA and England: 1/1, 2/2, 3/3, . . . , 12/12. This set of symbols corresponds to 12 different days of the year.

2 Let 6A and 6B represent the numbers. The product (6A)(6B) is equal to 36AB. Since 36AB = 504, AB = 504/36 = 14. If A = 1, 6A = 6 which violates the condition that neither of the numbers is 6. Then A = 2 and B = 7, or A = 7 and B = 2. In either case, the larger number is 6x7 or 42.

3 **Method 1.**
Find the dimensions of the large rectangle containing the walk and garden.

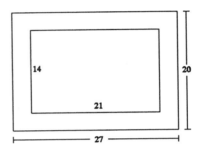

Area of the large rectangle is
    20x27 or 540 sq ft
Area of the garden is
    14x21 or 294 sq ft
Area of the walk is
    540 – 294 or 246 sq ft

Method 2.
Let A, B, C represent the areas as shown.

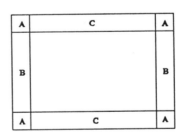

The area of the walk = 4A + 2B + 2C
A = 3x3 sq ft, B = 14x3 sq ft,
C = 21x3 sq ft.
Then the area of the walk
    = (4x9 + 2x42 + 2x63)
    or 246 sq ft.

4 **Method 1.**
Divide the difference between 1/2 and 1/3 by 3 since it takes three increases to go from 1/3 to 1/2. The result is 1/18.

$$\frac{1}{3}, \ \frac{?}{-}, \ \frac{?}{-}, \ \frac{1}{2}$$

$$\frac{\frac{1}{2} - \frac{1}{3}}{3} = \frac{1}{18}$$

The two missing numbers are $\frac{1}{3} + \frac{1}{18}$ and $\frac{1}{3} + \frac{2}{18}$, or $\frac{7}{18}$ and $\frac{8}{18}$.

Method 2.

Given:

$$\frac{1}{3}, \ \frac{?}{-}, \ \frac{?}{-}, \ \frac{1}{2}$$

Change to equivalent fractions with the same denominator:

$$\frac{2}{6}, \ \frac{?}{-}, \ \frac{?}{-}, \ \frac{3}{6}$$

Since we need three increases to go from the first to the fourth term and the numerators differ by only 1, multiply each fraction by 3/3:

$$\frac{6}{18}, \ \frac{?}{-}, \ \frac{?}{-}, \ \frac{9}{18}$$

The four terms are:

$$\frac{6}{18}, \ \frac{7}{18}, \ \frac{8}{18}, \ \frac{9}{18}$$

5 Denote the three given weighings in the given order as W1, W2, and W3.

1) Add □ to both sides of W1:   ○□ = △□□□

2) W2 is given as: ○□ = △◺

3) Then the right side of 1) and 2) are equal: △□□□ = △◺

4) Remove △ from both members of 3):   □□□ = ◺

5) W3 is given as: △ = ◺□

6) Substitute from 4) into 5):   △ = □□□□

7) Substitute from 6) into W1 (given):   ○ = □□□□□□